Options Trading

The Best Beginners Guide for All the Essential Information an Investor Needs to Understand on How the Options Market Works and How to Start Trading Options in 2019/2020.

Jim Livermore

Table of Contents

Introduction

Chapter 1: What are Stock Options?

Options: The Basic Concept

Two Classes of Options: Calls and Puts

Learning About Options Prices on the Market

Commissions

Chapter Summary

Chapter 2: Navigating the World of Options Trading

Call Options: In the Money

Call Options: Out of the Money

When is an option liquid?

Open Interest

Volume

Lower Open Interest Doesn't Mean Don't Trade

Call Option Examples

At the Money

Losing Money on Call Options

When to Trade Call Options

Trading Put Options

Put Option: In the Money

When to Invest in Put Options

How to Trade

Day Trading Options

Swing Trading Options

Do what works for you

Pros and Cons of Trading Call Options

Pros and Cons of Trading Put Options

Chapter 3: About Options Markets

Options are Derivatives Contracts

Options Exchanges

Options Clearing Corporation

Market Maker

The Options Industry Council

Virtual Trading Platforms

The Broker

Options vs. Stocks

Chapter 4: Tips and Avoiding Mistakes

Have Specific Goals

Keep a Trading Journal

Set a Profit Taking Amount Per Option Contract

Have a Stop Loss

Don't Let Emotion Rule Your Trades

Go Against the Herd

Use Alerts

Don't Try Making Up For Past Losses

Trading Illiquid Options

Chapter 5: Understanding The Options Greeks

Delta

Delta as a Probability

Gamma and How Delta Changes

Delta Values for the Put and the Call

Intrinsic and Extrinsic Value

Theta

Vega

Rho

Chapter 6: Options Strategies for Unchanging Prices: The Iron Condor and Iron Butterfly

The Iron Condor

Buying Back to Close

Iron Condor: Summary

Iron Butterfly

Summary: Profits From Stock Not Moving

Chapter 7: Trading Breakout Prices Using Strangles and Straddles

Strangle

Straddle

Summary: Strangles and Straddles

Chapter 8: Debit and Credit Spreads

Call Debit Spreads

Put Debit Spread

Put Credit Spreads

Call Credit Spreads

Buying Back to Close

Chapter 9: Selling Options

Covered Calls

Protected Puts

Selling Naked Put Options

Selling Naked Calls

Conclusion & Disclaimer

Introduction

Congratulations on purchasing *Options Trading* and thank you for doing so.

For most individual investors, options are a new way to make money through the stock market. Although they've been around for a long time, most people don't really understand what options are all about. In this book we will explain options for beginners in a way that will help you understand what options are, how they are traded, and how you can make profits from options.

Options are different than traditional investing. But the good thing about options is that they can help you earn profits without having to invest a lot of money. However, options are tricky if you have not educated yourself about how they work. That is one reason why reading this book is so essential. We will help you get started on the right foot so that you can trade options simply and easily without falling prey to the problems that options trading can create.

First we will begin with an introduction to stock options, explaining what they are and how they work. We will discuss the types of options and help you get acquainted with the jargon used in the options trading industry. We will explain how options compare with stock investing, and why options might be preferable for you when it comes to investing.

You'll learn why options provide massive leverage and how they actually save you money. As we learn about options, we'll demystify the "Greeks" and explain how to use them to make effective and winning options trades.

Finally we will cover different options trading strategies that can help to increase your odds of earning a profit while capping possible losses.

There are plenty of books on this subject on the market, thanks again for choosing this one! Every effort was made to ensure it is full of as much useful information as possible, please enjoy!

Chapter 1: What are Stock Options?

In this chapter we are going to introduce the basic concept of stock options. You will learn what options are, the two general classes of options, and the characteristics that any option has. We will also cover the language used to describe options in the industry.

Options: The Basic Concept

An option is a contract on some financial asset that involves buying or selling the asset at an arranged price. The benefit of this type of contract is that for a set time period it fixes the price of the asset over a given time period. The prototypical example used to illustrate this is a real estate contract. This is a bit hypothetical to illustrate how options work on the stock market, so bear with me and don't sweat the details as they related to the sale of a home.

Suppose that you have a house for sale, and someone is interested in the house but they are still uncertain about the purchase. Maybe the buyer will be moving to your town provided that they get a job at a particular place of employment. If they move to your town, they are certain to buy the house, but they don't want to commit to buying the house unless and until the job is finalized.

You could setup an option contract for 30 days on the house. The agreement might work as follows. It would give the buyer the option to buy the house for $250,000 within 30 days. This is an optional purchase for the buyer, they are not required to buy the house in 30 days. If they fail to buy the house in 30 days, the contract just expires and they lose their option to buy at that price.

For the seller of the option contract, it's not an option, it's an obligation. So if you enter into this contract, for that 30 days you can't take a different offer on the house, even if its for a higher price. If home prices in your area spike over the time period the contract is in force such that your house is now valued at $300,000, you still can't sell the house for that amount or for any price, unless and until the contract expires without the other party exercising their rights under the contract.

The buyer of the contract could transfer it to another party. If home prices are rising, other people might be interested in the contract, and since they could save a great deal of money on it with a home, they might be willing to buy the contract for a significant sum. So if the buyer finds out they are not going to get the job, they could let the contract expire worthless, or they could sell it to a third party for say $1,500. If home prices had risen making your home worth $275,000, even though they paid $1,500 for the contract, the ability to buy the house for $250,000 makes it worth it.

That is the options contract in a nutshell. For house all we have to do is substitute 100 shares of stock. So an options contract on the stock market has an underlying asset, which is 100 shares of stock and the basic options contract gives the buyer the right to buy 100 shares of stock on or before the expiration date at a fixed price.

The fixed price is called the strike price. The expiration date is very important, and there are various expiration dates for options on the stock market. A month is a typical length of time but there are also *weeklys*, which expire in a week, and there are LEAPS which expire in 1-2 years. You are going to find that there are options constantly expiring and available for investment at any time – so you will be able to find options to invest in that expire in a few days, in a week, in two weeks, in three weeks, a month, or whatever time frame you are interested in.

Two Classes of Options: Calls and Puts

There are two major classes or types of options contracts on the stock market. The type that we described in the last section is a *call option*. I introduced this type first because it is the easiest type to understand. To reiterate, a call options gives the buyer the option to buy 100 shares of stock at a fixed price on or before the expiration date.

But there is a second type of option, which is called a *put*. A put option gives the buyer the right to *sell* 100 shares of stock at a fixed price on or before the expiration date. Aside from being designated a call or a put, the language used to describe the characteristics of each option are the same, so the fixed price of sale is called the strike price for a put option as well.

When understanding these two different types of options, the main point to focus on is when and why you would want to use a specific type of option. We will consider call options first, because this is the most straightforward and common sense way to understand options and why they are useful.

I'm calling it common sense because a call option is beneficial when the stock price rises. If you buy a call option, you're hoping for the stock price to rise, and if the price does rise, the value of a call option on the marketplace increases. The more the stock rises in price, the more the value of the option increases. So prices of call options move with stock prices.

The reason that call options increase in value when the stock price increases is pretty straightforward. You've got an agreement that lets you buy shares of stock at a fixed price – the strike price. As the share price rises, the strike price becomes more attractive. If the share price goes above the strike price, then the option becomes very attractive – because now you can buy shares of stock at a discount.

Whether you are actually going to buy the shares isn't relevant. Someone is going to want to buy the shares, and so the value of the option will increase. If you are not interested in buying the shares of stock, it doesn't matter because you can sell the option to someone else, and earn a profit.

Now let's consider put options. The idea of having a contract that lets you sell 100 shares of stock at a fixed price seems mysterious at first, but put options are beneficial in a market of declining prices. So if the stock price is dropping, an investor can have some protection by using put contracts. That enables them to sell shares of stock at a fixed price that would be higher than the market price of the shares. For this reason, many investors buy put options to act as a kind of insurance on their stock holdings if there is reason to believe the stock may drop significantly in price.

Put options also let people *short the market*. This is a phrase used to describe a situation where a trader makes a profit from declining stock prices. This can be done by actually trading the stock in question, or by simply trading put options.

Let's look at the first situation. If a trader has reason to believe that the price of a certain stock is going to drop significantly, they can buy a put option that has a strike price near the current share price. In comparison to buying 100 shares of stock, a put option is going to be a small investment. If you are talking about a stock trading at $200 a share, buying 100 shares means a $20,000 investment, while you might be able to buy a put option for $100-$400. This is an important thing to note, if you consider the way stock traders short the market.

Traditional shorting of the market is actually a pretty high risk activity, because normally the way it's done is the trader will borrow the shares from the broker, and sell them on the market. If the price were to rise, the trader could lose a significant amount of money – because they have to return the shares to the broker.

There is a hoped for outcome. The trader borrows the shares from the broker, and then sells them on the market at the current stock price. Then the stock price drops, the trader buys them back at the reduced price, and then they return the shares to the broker. They pocket the difference that they got by selling the shares at the high price and then buying them back at a discount.

In order to participate in this type of trade, you need to have a large margin account with your broker so that you can borrow the shares. To borrow 100 shares trading at $200 a share you are talking about borrowing $20,000.

Put options allow you to do something similar for a few hundred dollars. Rather than borrowing from the broker, you invest a couple hundred bucks in the put option which secures your position should the stock price drop.

If the stock price were to drop, then you would buy them on the market, and then you can sell them to the originator of the put option at the strike price. Then your profit is the strike price x 100 – the lower market price – the cost of the put option.

We could put some specific numbers on this to help readers understand the concept. Disney stock is currently trading at

$132 a share. A put option with a strike price of $130 a share sells for $198.

So rather than buying 100 shares of Disney at $132 a share for a total of $13,200, or borrowing the shares, we spend just $198 to buy the put option. Of course, you are not going to do this randomly, for our thought experiment we are imagining that there is some reason to believe that the share price is going to drop significantly over the lifetime of the option contract, which expires in 30 days.

For the sake of example, suppose the stock dropped to $110 a share. That is a drop of $22 a share. You could buy the stock at $110 a share, for a total investment of $11,000 + $198 for the put option, setting you back $11,198. But since you own the put option, you could sell the shares at the strike price of $130 a share. That brings in $13,000. So your net profit would be:

Proceeds exercising the option − cost of buying the shares − cost of the option =

$13,000 - $11,000 - $198 = $1,802

A put option gives you the same power that shorting the stock does, but you are risking only a couple hundred dollars in the event things don't play out the way you are hoping.

And of course – there is a second path you can take. Rather than buying or selling shares, you can simply trade the option. Options prices are governed by certain mathematical formulas. You don't have to know what they are, but we can actually get a pretty accurate estimate of the price of a Disney put option should the stock price drop to $110. For our example we will suppose that this happens over a two week period. With two weeks left on the option contract, the price of a put option would rise to $1,998.

So we could simply sell the option, and ignore the shares of stock. This would give us:

$1,998 - $198 = $1,800

In this case we basically make the same profit that we would going through the exercise of buying and selling the stock. That isn't always going to be the case, but the example illustrates that you can profit from selling options *themselves* and not worrying about trading the stock at all.

This is why many people are options traders. An option allows you to control the stock and leverage its price movements without actually owning the stock at all. Notice that the $20 drop in share price is *magnified* in the price of the option. Later, when we learn about the "Greeks" we will get a precise notion of how options prices change with stock prices.

Learning About Options Prices on the Market

Now you understand the basic types of options that are available. We know that each options contract comes with a strike price and an expiration date. In this section we are going to learn about options pricing so that you understand the costs involved when you are looking to actually buy and sell them on the market.

The first thing to note about options pricing is that prices are quoted with three major factors taken into account. The first is the expiration date of the option. Options are grouped together by expiration date. So the first step in buying an option after picking the stock, is to find an expiration date of interest. Then you are going to see the options listed by strike price. So what you'll want to do after picking the stock and the expiration date, is find the desired strike price.

The price of the option that is the current market price is then listed on a price per share basis. So if you see an option priced for $1.50, you need to multiply that price by 100 to get the actual price that you have to pay in order to buy the option. In this case that would be 100 x $1.50 = $150.

The following image is taken from a trading app called Robinhood. The price of the option is circled on the right (incidentally, in the time that I wrote this the price dropped from $1.98 per share to $1.82).

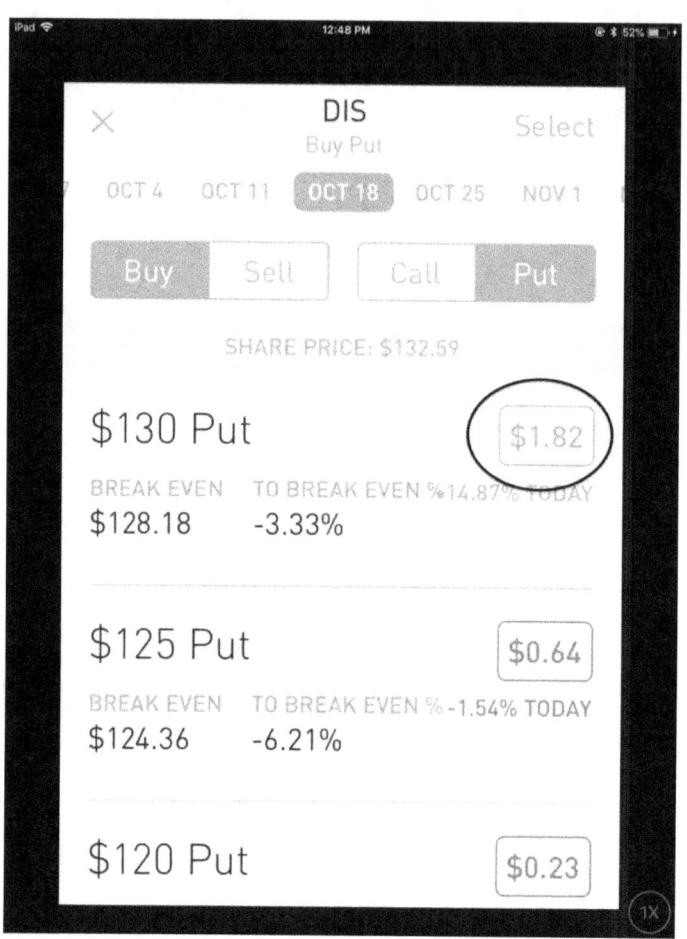

You might also see options prices quoted in a traditional format. Each option contract has its own ticker. Below, we have an example of a Disney option from Yahoo Finance, presented in this fashion.

DIS190920C00133000   2019-09-17 2:39PM EDT 133.00   3.30 3.35 3.60 0.00   -   24   0   134.57%

The ticker is:

DIS190920C00133000

The first three letters of an options ticker is the ticker for the stock that underlies the option. Following this the next 2 digits are the year, and then you have the month and day that the option expires. So the expiration date for this option is 9/20/19, or September 20th of 2019.

After the date, you will see a C or a P, indicating whether the option is a call or a put option, and in this example we have a C for call option. The information following this is the strike price information. Three decimal places are used, so this option has a strike price of $133. If it were $133.50, the ticker would read:

DIS190920C00133500

If it were a put option expiring on September 27th with a strike price of $125.50, it would be:

DIS190927P00125500

The price of the option is not reflected in the ticker, but if your broker displays tickers you will be able to find the price information alongside of it. These days most brokers display options pricing information in a more readable format the way that we saw above with the Robinhood app.

Commissions

Many brokerages charge commissions for entering into trades, and so this is an expense you may have to account for in your trading activity. Commission fees are typically pretty small relative to the size of trades, so they might be on the order of $5-$7. There are some brokers that might charge even lower commissions.

However, many brokers offer commission free trades. There are going to be many factors involved in choosing a broker, so whether it's worth it going for commission free trades is something you are going to have to evaluate as a part of a larger picture. If you are trading frequently having the ability to do commission free trades can be beneficial, but you might find paying a commission is worth it if you get a lot of additional benefits.

Chapter Summary

In this chapter we learned what an option contract is. Then we learned about the two types of stock options, calls and puts. We learned what the strike price is, and the importance of the expiration date and why you might want to sell put options. We also learned about options tickers and pricing. In the next chapter we are going to learn more about options expiration and some jargon about options that is commonly used in the field of options trading.

Chapter 2: Navigating the World of Options Trading

In this chapter we will cover basic options trading. For now, we will not cover selling options, a more advanced topic. In this chapter we will discuss simple examples of call and put options trading and some of the jargon used in the industry.

Call Options: In the Money

The terms "in the money" and "out of the money" are slang used by options traders to indicate whether an option is really worth something or not. It turns out that even out of the money options are worth something, but before we get to that let's learn what these terms mean and how different call options fit in with the definitions.

The first definition you need to know about is "in the money". A call option is in the money when the strike price of the call option is lower than the current share price. In other words a call option is in the money when you can buy the shares at a discount price relative to the market price.

To really be worth it, however, you need to understand how the breakeven price fits in. If the stock is trading at $101 a share, technically speaking a call option with a strike price of $100 a share is in the money. However, if you paid $2 per share for that option, then it is not really in the money, because you'd lose $1 a share exercising the option.

So from a practical standpoint, an option has to be positioned such that the market share price has risen enough to account not only for the strike price, but also the price paid to buy the call option. So you need to pay more attention to the breakeven price rather than the in the money price – if you are interested in buying the shares of stock.

Call Options: Out of the Money

So to summarize, a call option is in the money if the share price rises above the strike price. On the other hand, if the strike price is above the share price for a call option, then that option is said to be "out of the money". Out of the money options are less desirable than in the money options, and so they are priced at lower levels. The more in the money a call option, the more the option is worth.

However, you should not neglect out of the money options. If an option is a little bit out of the money, but the pricing trend is in its direction, the value of the option can still rise. So you can make profits from out of the money options, although it's a little bit trickier. Holding them overnight can also cause problems because options lose value due to time decay.

The key thing to remember about out of the money options is that they expire worthless. That is, if you hold an out of the money option through expiration, once the option expires it has zero value. That means your investment in the option is completely lost.

If you are going to trade out of the money options, then you should be sure to get rid of them as soon as possible. This is a good reason to be trading liquid options.

When is an option liquid?

Liquidity is one of the most important concepts in finance and trading. Simply put, liquidity is a measure (vague, but real) of how quickly you can convert something into cash.

A cashier's check is very liquid. Cash is 100% liquid. A bar of gold is pretty liquid because you can take it to a gold or coin dealer and sell it immediately for cash. Stocks are liquid, but less liquid than these items because you can't immediately access the cash you get from selling stocks (most brokers will make you wait a few days).

You can compare liquidity between different types of assets and within assets. To explain what we mean, let's focus only on options. Some options are going to be more liquid than others. No matter what, your broker is going to have rules on being able to get the cash out, but that isn't our concern when talking about the liquidity of options. Those rules are going to apply to all options.

Our concern here is how easy it is to buy and sell a particular option.

Options trading can move fast. In my own experience, I have seen options that I've purchased lose and gain $100 or more over a matter of 30-90 minutes. The rapid price movements of options coupled with the fact that they lose value through time decay every single day that passes means that when the time is right to get in and out of an options contract, you want to be able to do it right away.

So the concept of liquidity when it comes to trading options comes down to being able to buy and sell an option instantly. The market provides two important pieces of information that you can use in order to determine how liquid an option is.

Open Interest

Open interest is the number of contracts that are in existence for a given stock ticker, strike price, and expiration date. If you find that option A has an open interest of 1,250 for a strike price of $120 and an expiration date of October 1st, that means that there are 1,250 options contracts on the market for these values. If option B for a different stock only has an open interest of 85, that means there are hardly any traders interested in option B.

The higher the open interest, the easier the option is to trade and the faster your orders will get filled. Some stock tickers have very high levels of open interest, and so you can execute your trades instantly. Examples include the high tech companies or popular index funds like SPY. These may have some options with an open interest in the thousands.

While more is better, the minimum that is considered by professional traders is 100. So make a note to yourself as a rule that you will always check the open interest before entering a trade, and that you will only trade options with an open interest of 100 or greater.

Obviously an option with an open interest of 100 is going to take a lot longer to trade than one with an open interest of 2,400, but professional traders take 100 as large enough to ensure that you will be able to find a buyer or seller before there are large price movements that could wipe out your position.

Longer term options (LEAPS) might have smaller open interest but be worth buying anyway, because you can hold onto them longer. Remember that time decay becomes a huge issue for options that are approaching the end of their lifetime and it's not going to be as much of a factor for a longer term contract.

Volume

Volume is the number of times the option was traded. If the markets are open, volume tells you how many times its traded so far on that day. If the markets are closed, volume is the trading volume the previous business day. So if the open interest is 200 and volume is 500, it means there are 200 options contracts and they were traded 500 times on the last trading day.

More volume means that the option is more active, and it also means that it's going to be easier for you to get in and out of your positions when you need to.

Consider two examples. SPY is an index fund that tracks the S & P 500, which is an index consisting of the 500 largest companies on the stock market in the United States. Many traders like to trade SPY options because it's a high demand fund that provides a solid opportunity for traders. Looking at an example, an option that expires in two weeks that is in the money by $3 has an open interest of 5,920 and a trading volume of 1,310. With an open interest that high, you would have no problem trading this option – and you could probably sell it instantly.

The closer you get to the expiration date, you might find that the open interest begins decreasing, sometimes by large amounts. This is because sellers are closing out their contracts to avoid assignment (we will discuss what this specifically means in a later chapter).

Lower Open Interest Doesn't Mean Don't Trade

While there are no hard and fast rules, the 100 open interest level is generally followed by most professional traders, and it's a good rule for you to follow. That said, don't think that options with smaller levels of open interest are not worth trading as compared to options with open interest in the thousands.

While you might have to wait a little longer to execute a trade, they are often well worth trading. So just use 100 as a minimum cutoff and don't worry beyond that. If a stock with an option that has an open interest of 120 is trending strongly upward, you're going to be better off with that than you will with a different stock with an open interest of 2,500 that is stagnant.

Call Option Examples

The best time to trade call options is when a stock starts trending. A good example is SPY. If good GDP numbers come out, then you can make a good profit off call options on SPY. The key is getting in at the right point, which is why higher levels of open interest are good.

Sometimes an option will trend for a long time period. But remember with options you have time decay working against you. Let's illustrate with a few examples so that you can understand how this works. We will use a hypothetical stock with a share price of $200. First let's consider an in the money option with a strike price of $195, and say we buy it 14 days to expiration.

A call option would cost $6.10 per share under this scenario. That means that each option contract, covering 100 shares, would cost $610. If the share price rose to $203 on the same day, the option price for a call would jump to $810. So you can make significant profits on a single day.

But let's say that soon after you buy the option, the share price actually drops to $198. The option price would plummet to $487. So you'd lost a significant amount of money right out of the gate. But do you have the stomach to be a trader? The price might reverse, either the same day or a few days down the road.

If we hold out and wait a few days, and the price goes back up to $202 a share, the option price would now be $749. So we could sell it at a profit.

But let's look instead at holding it until 2 days before expiration. Suppose that at 11 days, it remains lower than $200 a share, so that we are still in a money losing situation. If we hold it all the way to 2 days, and it goes back up to $201 a share, the option price is now $602. So we can exit the position at a slight loss.

When you get close to expiration, the option is worth the difference between the share price and the strike price. That is related to the actual cash that would be generated by exercising the option. That would mean buying the shares at the strike price and then selling them at the market price.

If you don't intend to either keep the shares of stock or sell them after purchasing them, then you probably want to get rid of the option before it expires.

Now let's consider a different scenario. Five days to expiration, you buy an out of the money option. Once again we will start with a share price of $200. This time we will setup an out of the money call option. Remember that an out of the money call option has a strike price that is higher than the share price.

If the strike price is:

- $201: The option is worth $133.
- $202: The option is worth $96.
- $205: The option is worth $30.

Wow! So at a strike price of $205, we can get in on an option for cheap! Can we make profits? Let's look at each case.

First consider the $205 strike price. Suppose the same day, the stock rises from $200 a share to $203. That $30 option will rise in price to $99. Of course a $3 move is fairly large, but that certainly happens with stocks priced on the order of $200 a share.

So at least in theory, you could buy 10 options and make $690 in profit. But there might be day trading limitations. If you let it roll over another day and the price of the stock stays the same, the option price will drop to $81.

In that case, however, if the stock price rose to $203.25, the option price would jump to $90.

Options prices are governed by specific mathematical formulas, so these numbers are actually fairly accurate (but not exactly). They are hypothetical but they have been chosen to show that you can in fact trade out of the money options and earn profits on them. Academic articles on the internet give you bad advice – they say don't trade out of the money options.

The question really should be when to trade out of the money options. The time to trade out of the money options is to trade them when you expect or see a rising share price. Buying out of the money options at the beginning of a trend can save you a great deal of money, and you can still earn substantial profits.

Now let's consider the case of the $202 strike. In this situation if it goes through the same scenario, when the stock moves to $203.25 this option is in the money – and its price goes to $235. So you could sell it for a substantial profit.

The only situation to avoid when it comes to out of the money options is to not go out very far. If the option was $210, there would be little chance that the stock price would come anywhere near it. At 14 days to expiration with a share price of $200, you could buy it for $34, but at 4 days to expiration the option would be worth just $9, even with the share price rising to $203.25. So you'll want to pick strike prices that are reasonably close to the market price if you hope to earn profits trading out of the money options.

At the Money

An option can also be "at the money". This means that the stock price is exactly the same as the strike price. While this can and does happen, it doesn't happen that often, truthfully. At the money options are more responsive than out of the money options, with a delta of 0.50 or very close thereto. Later we will see that delta gives you the amount of movement you can expect in an options price for a given change in the share price. Options that are in the money are more strongly influenced by changes in share prices.

Losing Money on Call Options

Let's say for the sake of an example we buy a $200 strike price option that expires in 10 days on a stock trading at $200. A call option would cost $252. You would buy this option hoping that the share price is going to rise above the strike price.

Let's say that instead the share price languishes, moving between $199.50 and $200. Since it hasn't dropped much, we hold onto the option hoping things will move in our favor.

If instead the share price were to drop to $197 with 5 days left to expiration, the option price would plummet to $65. We would be out $187. Even if the share price only dropped to $198.75, the option would be priced at $122, still leaving you with a substantial loss.

It's important to realize that these kinds of losses can and do occur. It's important to do a thorough analysis of the situation before entering into a trade, and even with your best analysis you might still end up with heavy losses. Options trading is not magic, even though a lot of gurus are heavily marketing their "system" online claiming you can make constant profits. If someone sounds too good to be true, they probably are. A drop of $1.25 in share price for a stock priced at $200 is not very much – and it happens on a regular basis.

The key to successful options trading is not trading on a whim, carefully planning your trades, and knowing when to get out. The goal is to have more wins than losses over time that average out to profits. So you should not get too down if you have a loss or even a few losses in a row, they can be followed by several trading wins if you are planning your trades carefully and not just buying options to see what happens.

When to Trade Call Options

Hopefully these examples have illustrated how call options can work, both the good and the bad. The question is when is the best time to trade call options.

The first thing to look for is the start of a trend, especially if it's accompanied by some positive news about the company, or an overall upward trend in the stock market. This means that you should be devoting some amount of time to the financial news, and carefully following the stock charts of companies you are interested in trading with regard to options. That means looking at the stock itself, and not options prices. When you see signals of an uptrend forming in the stock, then that is the time to move in purchasing your options.

Options trading can be quickly. We illustrated a case where the value of an option could cause you substantial losses. But the thing is a stock priced at $198.75 could easily move to $202 that afternoon or the next day, and you could recover from your losses.

I have personally lost $100 in the course of an hour, only to move into a situation of $100+ profit a few hours later.

It can be difficult knowing for sure when the best times are to bail or to hold on. It's really impossible to know unless there are external factors that can be influencing the stock price. So if you are in a situation of losing money, but good news hits the airwaves about the company, then it is probably a situation that indicates you should hold on to at least recoup your losses and possibly move into a situation of profit.

But later we are going to lay down some trading rules that you should follow. In most cases, trying to figure out what is going to happen using a crystal ball is not the best way to approach trading. You should have rules that guard against losses, and that means having a maximum loss per option that you are willing to accept.

Bailing out when these losses occur does mean that sometimes you are going to miss out on some recoveries. However, most of the time it's going to minimize your losses. It's better to minimize your losses and then live for another day. There are always new trades to get into.

Trading Put Options

Stocks are always going up and down, and while most stocks are trending with the market, even when they are going one way there are going to be outliers that are going in the opposite direction. And sometimes the market overall is tanking. But the beauty of options is that you can easily profit either way. Put options allow you to profit from market downturns.

Let's return to our example of a stock that is priced at $200 a share, and we are going to look at put options this time around. In this situation we would be doing so because there is reason to believe that the stock is going to decline.

At 14 days to expiration, a $200 put option which is at the money (the strike price is equal to the share price) would cost $296. Let's say that in 7 days there is an earnings call, and there are expectations that the earnings call is not going to be a good one. This is an opportunity to invest in put options, but do keep in mind that there is some risk involved here. If the earnings call turns out better than expected, the share price may not drop.

At 7 days left to expiration, let's say the earnings call turns out to be worse than expected. In situations like this – which do happen frequently – the stock can drop a large amount. A drop of $20, or even $40 a share overnight is not unheard of. So for our example let's say the share price drops $33. This could send the price of the put option all the way up to $3,229!

So a situation like that can bring you substantial profits from your bet against the company. Of course betting right is risky business, so don't expect things to move your way that dramatically all the time or even very often.

Sometimes the market might not react much. If the stock only dropped $5 a share, the put option at 7 days to expiration would be worth $546. Of course since we bought the option for $296, this is still a good profit.

Put options can be useful in many circumstances. Sometimes people are just getting out of a given stock. You can study technical analysis and learn when stock is overbought. This usually means that share prices are going to drop as investors start getting out of the stock. This can be a good time to buy put options and earn some money.

The key factor here, of course, is paying attention. You have to know what is going on with trading and also with the financial news. That can include not only company news but also political news and anything that can impact the markets overall movements, like job reports and so on. That is one reason that many traders like to focus on trading options against index funds. In order to make educated guesses about price movements, you only have to follow political and macroeconomic news. General moods can move SPY leading to profits in either direction.

This requires some flexibility in your thinking processes. We are conditioned to think in terms of earning profits from increasing prices. As an options trader, you need to be flexible so that you are able to earn profits no matter which direction the market moves. I always encourage brand new options traders to get in the habit of buying some put options to get a feel for how it works in real time, so that they can learn how to earn profits no matter which way things are going. Ridding yourself of the bias toward increasing stock prices is something you need to do as an options trader.

Put Option: In the Money

Put options work in the opposite way as compared to call options, and so the notions of "in the money" and "out of the money" are reversed. In the case of a put option, we say that it is in the money if the share price is *below* the strike price.

So if you have a put option with a strike price of $220 but the share price is $200, that put option is in the money. The reason is you could buy shares of stock at $200 and then exercise the put option and sell them for a profit of $20 a share (not considering the cost to buy the option). In contrast, with a share price of $200, a call option with a strike price of $220 would be far out of the money.

If there were 30 days left until the option expired, and the share price was $200 with a strike price of $220, the call option would only be worth $4! However, the put option in this case would be worth $2,013!

A put option that has a strike price below the share price is out of the money. Now say that instead, the share price is $220 and the strike price is $200. This time the call is going to be priced at $2,032, and the put option is going to be virtually worthless at $18. But if the stock price were to drop to $208, the put option would gain in value, moving up to $152.

If the options are at the money, they are going to be priced about the same. With 30 days left until expiration, and $200 strike prices when the share price is $200, the put option and the call option are both going to be priced at about $432. That makes sense because the stock could move either way, and so both are going to be worth the same in the marketplace.

When to Invest in Put Options

You can invest in put options any time the market is declining for a specific stock (or generally, if you are trading options against index funds). This can be done as things are going – so you can jump into a downward trend as it's happening. Or if you have information about upcoming events that leads you to believe that stock prices are going to be dropping in the near future, you can buy put options to short the stock.

How to Trade

Trading straight put and call options is very easy. You simply find the stock that you are interested in, and then pick an expiration date and strike price that you feel are good values to use. Generally speaking longer time frames until the expiration of the option are better, for two reasons. The first reason is that longer time frames mean that the option has more time value left. This gives you more time to have things move in your favor before exiting the trade. Second, in most circumstances it's better to sell options that have more time remaining on the contract, because a longer expiration date is going to be more interesting to buyers, since they will feel they have time to have the stock move in such a way that they can make profits.

That doesn't mean that you can't make money trading options that only have a short time left. I've done it and many traders even trade on the last day or two to earn profits. If the stock price is moving, any option can gain value (or lose it as well). The thing to watch out for in this case is making sure that the open interest and volume are high so that when you need to exit the position you can sell the option. Unless you are planning to buy the stock and the option is in the money, you don't want to be holding onto options too close to expiration.

Trading involves simply buying the call or put options you feel are a good trade, and then holding them until the price moves in such a way that you have earned the kind of profit that you are hoping to make on the trade. It's really that simple – but trading options is harder and trickier than this sounds. For this reason most professional options traders don't just buy calls and hope to make profits from increasing share prices.

Instead, they use advanced strategies. Let's just think about the fact that we can buy call and put options. You could start buying them in different combinations in order to ensure that you are going to earn profits. For example, if you were betting that the stock price was going to rise, you could buy an in the money or close to at the money call option, but you could also buy an out of the money put option as a little bit of insurance in case your bet was wrong. So the put option could focus as a hedge.

That could even lead to making profits on both ends. Just for an example, suppose that the share price is $200. You could buy an at the money put option (strike price = $200) for $437. You could also buy an in the money call option with a strike price of $197.50 for $571. In the event that the share price goes up to say $202, then the call option would rise to $699, while the put option would drop to $342. So you gained $128 on the call option but lost $95 on the put. You could sell both options and take a modest profit.

This example illustrates that you can hedge with options, but at the expense of profit. That is we made less profit than we would have just buying the call option by itself. Is that a tradeoff worth making? Sometimes it might be, but as we will see in later chapters, there are specific strategies that have been developed that will help you make set profits and minimize losses. These strategies are known as limited risk and limited reward strategies. Professional options traders use strategies of that time in order to build an income that they can rely on over time, by increasing the probability that their trades are winning trades.

This recognizes the fact that even an experienced trader is going to have problems consistently picking winning call or put options on their own.

Let's return to the scenario above. Of course this approach carries a lot of risk, but when the stock price went up you could sell the call option and then hold onto the put option. The idea behind this would be that you might be able to profit from both options. We are not really talking about stock pricing moves that are all that dramatic, and the reality is that the stock market is always going up and down a lot over short time periods. So what you could try to do is sell the call option when the stock is nearing a peak in pricing, but hold the put option on the bet that the stock is going to drop back down, at least a bit, and increase the value of the put option.

Once again let's say that the stock price rose to $202. Then the following day, suppose it drops to $201.25. The put option would be priced at $367 – so we recovered some of the loss that we incurred earlier. If the stock continued dropping, say to $200.80, then the put option would rise to $387. At either point, we could have sold the put option and recovered some of the previous losses, increasing our overall net profit.

Now suppose the next day it drops to $199. In that case, the put option would rise in value to $468.

The point of these scenarios is to get you thinking about the possibilities of entering into more complicated trades. There are a lot of gurus going around the internet claiming that they pick winning call options all the time, but the chaotic nature of the stock market makes this unlikely. But by entering into more complicated trades, you can increase your odds of making money, and sometimes you can make substantial profits.

Here is a scenario similar to one I actually engaged in myself. Suppose that the stock is trading at $186 a share, and we buy a call option with a strike price of $188 and a put option a strike price of $184. There are five days left to expiration.

The call option will cost $85, and the put option will cost $83. So we are about even on both sides of the market price. Now suppose the stock drops to $184 a share. The put option increases to $163. So we can sell it and take a $80 profit. At this point the call option is $37, having lost a significant amount of money. But we have reason to believe that the share price is going to turn around and go up – and probably exceed the strike price of the call. So we hold onto it.

Over the course of a couple of hours, the share price rises to $187, $188, and then to $190. Now the call is worth $287. Then it goes to $190.50, and we sell the call option for $322.

Our profit on the call option is $322-$85 = $237, and we also earned a profit of $80 on the put option, for a total profit of $317. Not bad for a days work! Of course finding trades that work in this manner is not something that you are going to be able to do all the time, but it does happen and it shows how you can make money quickly from the chaotic price moves that happen all the time on the markets.

Day Trading Options

In order to take advantage of the large price moves that happen throughout the day, you may want to day trade options at least some of the time. The reason is simple. Day trading options allows you to take advantage of the price swings that happen on the markets daily without holding options overnight and losing value to time decay. Remember that with each passing day, the option will lose some value on that basis alone, although other factors are in play that might rise above time decay causing the options to gain in value on the following day.

But let's imagine that share prices are remaining constant. We'll also assume for the sake of illustration that everything else including implied volatility (more on this later if you have not heard of the concept before) are remaining constant. Suppose a stock is trading at $300 a share. We'll use an at the money option with a strike price of $300. The price of a call option will move as follows, simply due to time decay.

- 30 Days: $655
- 20 Days: $535
- 10 Days: $378

- 5 Days: $267
- 3 Days: $207

Time value works against options traders. If the option is out of the money, it takes on an outsized role in causing value to drop as the days pass.

The problem with day trading, however, is that you can only do so many day trades over any five day period (that being five business days). So unless you want to open a day trading account, you have to be careful about using day trades and only use them sparingly. Four day trades in any five day period, where the period is five consecutive trading days (so weekends don't help) result in a day trader designation.

A day trader has to open a margin account, with a deposit of $25,000 according to the regulations in the United States. A margin account is one that allows you to borrow money in order to do trades.

For some people, this may not be an obstacle. Are you willing to sink $25,000 into your account in order to day trade options? For some people, this might be worth doing.

It is certainly a plausible scenario, and once you open a day trading account, as long as you maintain the account in good standing, you can day trade as much as you like under those   circumstances.

In my view this is worth at least setting up, so that when you need to day trade options in order to make profits you will have that ability. Keep in mind everyone has the ability, but only up to 3 day trades per 5 business days. If you open a day trading account then you will be able to unlimited numbers of day trades.

So what is a day trade? That is simply buying a security and then selling it before market close on the same day.

Keep in mind that trading two different options doesn't amount to a day trade. So if you buy an option on Apple with a strike price of $199 and then later that same day buy another option on Apple with a strike price of $198, and then sell the option with the strike price of $199, you have only made one day trade.

So for a day trade each option is a unique security, so that means the same strike price and the same expiration date. If you buy 10 options with the same strike price and expiration date you might not be able to sell all of them on the same day, depending on the brokerage rules.

Day trading options can be very lucrative, but this is a full-time activity and it can be very high pressure. In order to have success with this style of trading, you will have to be paying close attention to the markets all day long until you close out all of your trades. Some people will enjoy this, but other simply won't be able to because of other commitments they have in their life such as a full-time job. You might also not be able to put $25,000 into your trading account, or enjoy the pressure of having to make quick trading decisions. But this is something fun and exciting for some people.

Swing Trading Options

Swing trading is a style of trading financial assets that relies on large price movements or "swings" that occur over time. With stocks, swing trading is a popular strategy. It is not as high pressure as day trading and you can do it without a margin account or any deposit requirements. The basic idea is to buy at a relative low point in prices, and wait for the stock price to "swing" to a high pricing level where you can sell and take your profits. It can also be used to short the market, so you would enter a position at a pricing peak and then exit the position when the price swings back down to a low price.

Swing traders hold their positions overnight, and then trade over the course of days or even weeks.

It could be a natural fit to options trading of straight calls and puts. The basic process of trading only calls, for example, is not that different from swing trading because you are simply looking to buy low and sell high. Conversely, with put options you are shorting the market, as a swing trader could do when the market is at a high and then "swinging" down to a low price.

The only difference is swing traders don't have to worry about expiration dates and time decay, but options traders have to. That doesn't mean that you can't effectively swing trade using options, you can. But you have to account for time decay in your trades. You might consider swing trading using LEAPS since they are less susceptible to time decay over the time periods of interest, but they could also move substantially with large price swings of the underlying stock. LEAPS will not move in the same magnitude as options close to expiration when stock prices change, but they do still move a large amount. You can look for a 65 cent per share change on a LEAP for every dollar change in the stock, for example. But the important thing about LEAPS is that the time decay is very small, so unlikely to have much impact if any on the price.

That means that if you are really going to approach options trading from a swing trading perspective, trading LEAPS can be a way to do that. They can also save you a large amount of money while providing a much higher return on investment as compared to trading stocks. As an example, you could buy in the money calls on Apple at $3700. Sounds like a lot until you consider that the 100 shares underlying those call options would cost more than $20,000 at the time of writing.

Do what works for you

There are no rules for trading. So you should pick a style and goals that work best for you and your personality style, as well as with your ability to make financial commitments to trading without putting yourself at too much risk.

Pros and Cons of Trading Call Options

Trading call options is the common sense way to trade, and they are easy to understand. When the stock price goes up the value of the call option goes up. So it's a straightforward way to get involved in options trading. It's also a good way to get started and get a feel for the options market before getting involved in more sophisticated strategies. In the beginning you can start by just trading small priced options. Go for some options for well-known but lower priced stock, such as AMD. The stock trades for around $30 a share or so, and you can get in the money call options for around $125.

After you get comfortable doing a few trades on stocks like AMD, you can move up to higher priced and faster moving stocks like Facebook, Apple, and SPY. With more active stocks the prices are going to be moving faster, and there are going to be more opportunities for profits.

The cons of trading call options by themselves are mainly focused on two areas. Prices can suddenly go against you. If you are trading something like Facebook, and you wait too long, a small price shift, going down 75 cents or a dollar, can put you in a situation where you lose a lot of money quickly. The trick to avoiding this is getting out of the trade at the right time by selling your options when you are making a profit, or if they start heading in the other way getting out before things get too bad.

Another con of trading call options by themselves is time decay. If you don't plan things right time decay can cost you a lot of money as well and make it harder to recover from losses. Dealing with time decay simply involves having awareness of it and planning head.

Pros and Cons of Trading Put Options

On the pro side, put options give you more flexibility for earning money from stock price movements. They make it easy to short the market, and they are relatively straightforward to understand. That said, some new traders will find them a little bit confusing. Just like with call options, I recommend that you start with a few small trades with put options so that you can understand how they work, getting a feel for it in real time, but without putting much money on the line.

The cons of put options is that it's a little counter-intuitive for most people to be thinking of making money when the stock market is declining. This can lead to trading mistakes. However, that is something you can deal with by practicing. You can even start getting acquainted with put options by following market movements for different stocks without actually entering into any trades. That way you can start learning how to recognize opportunities to profit from stock market declines, and train yourself to think in terms of shorting the market. Of course it isn't a requirement that you trade by shorting the market, but doing so will help you gain a bit of flexibility.

Chapter 3: About Options Markets

In this chapter we are going to introduce you to the options markets. In your trading, some of the concepts involved in this chapter are background material that won't impact your actual day-to-day trading. We will also talk about brokers and commissions as well, which is going to be more impactful. But the lessons of this chapter will be understanding the structure of the options market and who is involved.

Options are Derivatives Contracts

Options are a type of derivative contract. You may have first heard about "derivatives" during the 2008 housing market crash. But don't let the term scare you. *Derivative* simply means that the value of a financial security is derived from an underlying asset. In the case of options, the value of the option is derived from the underlying shares of stock.

Options Exchanges

Just like stocks, options are traded on exchanges. There are many options exchanges. The largest options market is owned by NASDAQ, which as you probably know is a stock market that is mainly made up of technology stocks. NASDAQ actually owns six different options exchanges. These include the Nasdaq Options Market, PHLX, BZX, Gemini, Mercury, and ISE. Together, the six options exchanges owned by NASDAQ make up about a third of total options trading. Another major options exchange is CBOE/BATS.

CBOE stands for the Chicago Board Options Exchange. Chicago is generally seen as the center of options trading, but there are also options exchanges in Boston and New York. ISE stands for the international securities exchange. It was developed in the late 1990s as a fully electronic exchange.

As a trader, the options exchanges are totally hidden from you. Trading options, like trading stocks, will be presented to you in an electronic format that is completely unified, and the actual exchange where the option is bought or sold is invisible. Your broker creates the interface between you and the options exchanges. So while it may be good to at least know about the options exchanges, this is not something you have to become an expert on in order to trade options or to make a profit trading options. You won't even be aware of the exchanges themselves as you go about your business.

Options Clearing Corporation

The options clearing corporation or OCC is an organization that issues and guarantees options contracts. The OCC is regulated by the U.S. Securities and Exchange Commission or SEC. The OCC manages transactions involving call and put options. They are also involved with futures contracts. The main function of the options clearing corporation is to ensure that the obligations outlined in options contracts are fulfilled by working with brokers. The organization also helps provide regulatory oversight of the options markets to help manage risk.

Market Maker

Options market makers are under contract with options exchanges to help provide liquidity in the options markets. These are professional traders that are paid by the exchanges to fulfill this role. They can be large institutional traders or even individuals. The main purpose of market makers is to ensure that retail traders are able to trade options. Market makers will often take the other side of your trades. They maintain a large inventory of financial assets of their own, and often use actual stock trades to hedge their risk in taking options trades that have a certain probability of being a losing trade. Market makers are viewing the markets in a completely different way than individual traders such as yourself view the market. This is because they are not focused on individual trades. They are focused on the aggregate of large numbers of trades and overall probabilities. When you are trading, you aren't going to know who takes the other side of the trade and it's not really relevant. It might be another retail trader, it could be an institution or it might be the market maker. Your only focus when trading is on the performance of the stock, and entering and exiting trades in a way that works for your personal situation. Market makers have huge portfolios of options contracts that are known as "inventory". If you are trading a low volume option, the market maker can help keep the market liquid by taking the other side of the trade.

The Options Industry Council

The Options Industry Council or OIC is an educational organization. It is sponsored by many options exchanges, and it's main purpose is to educate the public about options trading. The organization maintains a website for this purpose located at optionseducation.org where you can find courses on options trading as well as data associated with options trading. They also have an online store where you can buy videos, books, and software. This site is highly recommended for use to further your education in options trading. You should use these reliable and official course materials rather than relying on online gurus who have other, sometimes, ulterior motives.

Virtual Trading Platforms

If you are a true beginner, you might consider signing up with a broker that offers a demo trading platform. This will allow you to engage in demo options trades so that you can gain experience without risking any money. For all intents and purposes, the demo trades operate as real trades with the exception of real money being on the line, so you can go through trades and learn how things work with no real risk. Since options trading can be quite tricky and different from stock trading, using this procedure is highly recommended, at least for a short time period. Many people are impatient and want to dig into real trading right away, but if you prepare yourself by spending a few weeks or a month using a demo trading platform, you are going to be better off than someone who starts out the gate risking their own funds. Do some research online to find a broker that has a practice trading platform. Some examples include think or swim which is operated by the famous stock broker TD Ameritrade, and another one you can use is run by a company called Tasty Works.

The Broker

Just like you need a broker to trade stocks as an individual investor, you need a broker to trade options. Since options are closely associated with the stock market, the same brokers that are used to trade stocks are involved in options trading.

What is a broker? A broker is simply a middleman. As we mentioned at the start of this chapter, there are many different options exchanges. As an individual trader, you are not going to go through the work of finding where a specific option is traded and then go trade on the exchange.

Instead, everything is hidden from you by the broker who does the actual legwork. Of course these days everything is managed electronically, and so the broker will present you with the options exchanges as if it were one single, unified market. They play the role of acting between you as the individual trader and the exchange and whomever takes the opposite side of the trade.

With today's computational power and fully electronic trading, everything runs seamless. Behind the scenes, you place an order with your broker, and the broker actually carries out the trade on your behalf. Since the broker is doing work for you, they will often charge a fee for placing each trade that is called a commission. Not all options brokers charge commissions, and they make money in other ways.

The broker will provide a software interface that you can use for options trading. Some brokers provide a basic interface that will allow you to look up options and place your trades, while others will also include the ability to do in-depth analysis. These days most brokers make their interface available through the internet on desktop computers, or as mobile applications for tablets and mobile phones.

Finding a good balance between features offered by the broker and fees like commissions is important. If you are using a broker that does charge commissions, this is going to be something that you have to figure into all of your trades when calculating profits and losses.

Tasty Works is one of the most popular options trading platforms. It was started by pit traders from the Chicago exchanges, and so it's run by people that really know the business. They also have an associated educational network called tasty trades, that helps educate people and keep them informed, often including interviews with successful options traders. Tasty works charges small commissions, on the order of $1 per option contract. Later we will learn about more complicated options strategies that involve multiple options in a single trade. Each option is known as a "leg". So if you have 2 options in a single trade, that is a 2-leg trade, while a trade involving 4 options has four legs. When selecting a broker you are also going to want to know about any charges associated with legs. Tasty works will charge a maximum of $10 per leg. Single leg trades are $1 each, but as of 2018 the company allows you to open 100 calls or puts for just $10. As of 2018 they also lowered their prices for 100 vertical 2 leg options to $20, and 100 4 leg trades were capped at $40. So the price of $10 per leg is for 100 options contracts. They also only charge commissions on opening an options trade and there is zero commission charged on closing options trades.

Robinhood has become a very popular trading platform. While you can access it through a desktop computer, it's mainly designed to run as a mobile app. Robinhood is very popular because it has a clean, simple trading interface and it also charges zero commissions. They make their money through other ways, such as offering a "gold" membership for a monthly fee that has more features.

Many experienced traders don't like Robinhood because it has some downsides. The most important downside for most traders is that it has limited information available as far as tools used for analysis. However, you can get that type of information elsewhere, so you might look at it as a tradeoff that you are willing to accept in order to get commission free trades.

Traditional stock brokers offer options trading as well. These include Charles Schwab, E*Trade, and TD Ameritrade.

Ultimately the broker you choose is a personal decision, so you should evaluate each broker you may be interested in and find the one you prefer, rather than doing what others tell you to do.

Once you find your broker, you can fund your account. This is done by linking a bank account to the account maintained by your broker and depositing some funds into the account. You can trade options contracts one at a time, so you only need to fund an account with a couple hundred dollars in order to get started. I advise that beginners start slowly and small, don't jump in and buy 20 call options right away. Do one contract at a time so that you can learn how to trade options before putting significant money at risk.

Options vs. Stocks

The main advantage of options over stocks is that options provide leverage and massively higher return on investment. We touched on this earlier. You can invest a much smaller amount of money and earn profits that are similar in magnitude to what you would earn actually trading 100 shares of stock, but without having to put thousands of dollars at risk. For those who don't have thousands of dollars to put at risk trading, options offer a way for them to take advantage of price swings in the market.

Consider a stock trading at $200 a share. If you were to buy 100 shares of stock, that would require an investment of $20,000. Now suppose that the stock rises by $2 a share. That would give you a total of $200 in profit, not accounting for commissions. So you could sell the 100 shares and take your profits. Of course $200 profit from one trade is a good take.

If you were to buy an option, it would cost $437 to buy an at the money option ($200 strike price) with 30 days to expiration. A $2 rise in the stock price over 2 days would mean the option would rise to $525, so you could sell it for an $88 profit.

The ROI on the stock trade would be:

ROI (for stock trade) = ($20,200 - $20,000)/$20,000 x 100 = 1%

The ROI for the options trade would be:

ROI (for options trade = ($525-$437)/$437 x 100 = 20%

That shows the power of leverage that options provide. Of course you need to keep in mind that losses as well as gains are magnified by options, but this shows the power to make profits on smaller investments. In fact if we traded 3 options contracts, we'd have a profit of $264, larger than that from buying the stock. To do that we'd only need to invest $1,311, a fraction compared to the $20,000 we'd have to invest to make that kind of profit using a stock trade.

For those who have the funds available, trading stocks might be preferred because it can be more straightforward and familiar. But if you would rather make the same levels of profits while risking less money, or you don't have the funds required to make large stock trades like that, options offer an advantage.

The cons of options trading as compared to stock trading are mainly centered around the fact that options can move quickly in price and the trading can be tricky. Stocks also have the advantage of not coming with an expiration date. If the stock was languishing, you could hold onto 100 shares of stock as long as you need to in order to make a profit. With options trading it's something that you have to get in and out of quickly, and you have to be aware of the expiration date.

We can summarize the pros of options vs. trading stocks in the following:

- There is far less capital required to trade options as compared to stocks to make equivalent profits.
- Options provide a much better return on investment as compared to stocks.
- Options are fixed loss investments. The total loss you can incur is the price of the option. Losses on stocks can be much larger.

- Options offer flexible ways of trading, and it's easier to profit from price declines as opposed to shorting stock.
- As we will see in later chapters, it's possible to enter trades with options that do things that are not possible trading stocks.
- Options require less startup capital.
- Options have less risk from "gap openings", which are fast price changes that can wipe out a day trading account at market opening, if the trader had held a position overnight.
- Options offer flexibility, since you can trade over different time frames.

Chapter 4: Tips and Avoiding Mistakes

In this chapter we are going to look at some general tips to help you to become a successful options trader. We will also look at some common mistakes to avoid. Following this advice and putting it into practice is going to be strictly up to you, however those who take this advice to heart are going to be better traders than those who ignore it. This advice is based on the experience of actually going out and trading options, so we can save those who are willing to study the trouble of having to make mistakes that others have learned from already.

Have Specific Goals

The first thing to realize about trading options is that you should treat it as a serious business, even if you are only planning on trading on a part-time basis. After all, real money is involved so why do otherwise?

Any successful business is going to be built around specific goals. You need to have an idea of where you are going and be able to chart your progress along the way. With that in mind you should start with a goal for an amount of income that you want to earn from options trading. Start with a monthly target, rather than an annual target. That way you can adjust your numbers as you gain experience and develop your trading skills. You can also target weekly goals instead.

Over the long term, you should have an annual income in mind. Are you looking to replace your job, or make a certain amount of money from trading options? Or are you simply looking to earn some extra money?

Depending on your financial goals, you are going to need to figure out how much time you are willing and able to devote to trading. If your goal is to make $100k a year trading options, then working on it 5 hours a week is probably not going to be sufficient. So keep a realistic perspective on how much time you are going to devote to trading and how much money you intend to make. Keep in mind that you don't have to get everything done in a single step and you can grow into your ultimate goals. So if you want to become a full-time trader making a six-figure income, you might start small, only trading a few hours a week with a goal of making $1,000 a month right now. Then as you gain experience, you can set new goals.

Keep a Trading Journal

Of course the computer and your broker will keep a record of your trades, but one thing I have found is that those who are more likely to attain success are those who keep a trading journal. Get a notebook and record your trades, and keep a running tally of your income. Each time you open a new trade, enter it in your notebook. Then record it in your notebook when you exit the trade, and note the net profit or loss on the trade.

It is important to track wins and losses in your notebook. One of the bad habits people have while engaging in an activity like options trading is the winning trades stick to their memory, but oddly enough they seem not to remember the losing trades. It's important to keep a running tally that includes your *net* income as well as a win-loss count of your trades. If you win 2 trades but lose 10 trades, that is an indication that you have some learning to do. Keeping a trading journal where you record every single action that you take can help you be honest with yourself as well as help you keep a reliable record of your trading activities. That way you will know where you really stand.

Set a Profit Taking Amount Per Option Contract

Each trade that you enter into should have clearly defined exit criteria. That means that you should have a fixed profit level that you use to exit trades. With options, it is very easy for a good trade to suddenly go bad. Remember that options magnify small price movements in the stock, and so you can lose money just as fast as you make money.

For that reason, it's better to set a fixed profit level per option and per trade that gets you in the habit of taking fixed dollar amounts that add up over time. All too often, when it comes to options trading holding on while you hope to make $100 or more on a single trade can lead to a $50 loss instead. Or maybe if you are lucky, you will break even.

Two things to remember while options trading are the following. First, there is always another trade around the corner. Think of all the new options contracts that you can find to trade each and every single day. Second, remember that options are time limited. So holding on hoping to make more profits is not the best approach.

Small dollars add up as well. Remember that many people become millionaires by saving small amounts of money. In the world of options trading, you might be thinking in terms of one contract at a time, but as you gain experience and get better judgement about what is a good trade and when to enter and exit your trades, you can move up to trading multiple contracts at a time.

A good rule to set is an exit rule when you earn profits. It should be at least $30 per contract, but at most $100 per contract. While it might not be exciting to make say $50 on an options trade, try imagining doing that many times per day instead. You can get to the point where you are trading 10 or 20 options at the same time, and so you can make $500 or $1,000 per trade. Over time, you can do that more frequently and trade even more contracts simultaneously.

But what happens when you set a $30 or $50 take profit level per options contract is that you increase the probability that you are going to be able to exit a trade in a profitable state. You also get out of the practice of "winging it" as you are trading. Successful options traders are disciplined and have specific plans that they execute. You can't expect to be a successful options trader if you are acting "on the fly".

As I've said and I want to emphasize again, I routinely see options hit a profitable zone when you have made $50 or so on a contract. If you wait it out, there is a strong probability that you are going to see that go south on you. It's really not worth waiting around for a larger profit level. Yes, sometimes that will happen but remember the market maker – they are playing on the probabilities of the options market. You should do that as much as possible too.

Have a Stop Loss

A stop loss order with stocks is a fixed amount of losses per trade that the trader is willing to accept. Generally speaking, financial advisors say that you should not risk more than 2% of your account per trade. With stocks, you figure out 2% of your account size, and then divide that by the number of shares you are trading. Then you can place a limit order, which is a type of order on stocks that only executes if the price specified is reached. In this case, the limit order would be a sell order that would automatically sell your shares if the price dropped by the amount specified.

You can do the same concept here, but the way I do it is a fixed dollar amount per options contract. You have to be careful with this, because with options contracts there is always a good chance of a turn around. Like the take profit level, this is some value you are going to have to figure out for yourself. The idea is to be able to get out of options trades that don't look good, but you want to get out without losing the entire amount that you paid for the option.

But you also have to consider that options can quickly turn around and move the other direction. Remember that a $0.50 move on the stock against the direction you are hoping for can mean a $40 or even $50 loss on your option, and that is not much price movement. So setting some small level like $10 would not be realistic. You have to give the stock some breathing room to move up and down. I generally pick a level of about $100. You can also look for a consistent downtrend. That is, if the stock keeps dropping with no end in sight, you might get out of the trade rather than let it carry through to the next trading day, leaving you with even more losses due to time decay.

Don't Let Emotion Rule Your Trades

The previous two tips help with the biggest problem of them all, letting emotion rule your trades. If prices on a financial market are dropping by significant amounts, this can get people into trouble because they will panic at the thought of large financial losses. When that happens, they exit trades too soon, and they end up missing out on later price gains. And as we've mentioned before, this can happen with rising prices as well. If you don't have a take profit rule that you stick to, you can end up holding onto your assets for too long. That can mean at best reduced profits, but it can also mean breaking even or having to exit your trades at a loss. So you want to stick to your profit rule no matter what. Don't hold on after its reached the profit level hoping that you are going to be making larger and larger profits.

Go Against the Herd

When the markets are dropping, don't sit on the sidelines. Don't move into cash. Remember that as an options trader you have an level of flexibility that stock traders (generally) don't have. That means that bear markets and dropping stock prices are an opportunity to earn profits.

Use Alerts

If you can sign up for email alerts with your broker or through another service, this is something you can do in order to ensure that you are staying on top of your trades. You can use alerts so that you can keep up with changing stock prices, whether it's getting into a trade at the right moment or exiting your trades. Alerts sent to your email inbox or as text messages can help you keep up with things without having to be directly following the market all day long.

Don't Try Making Up For Past Losses

Besides trading on emotion, another mistake beginners make is trying to make up for past losses by doubling or tripling up on the next trade. You need to maintain a disciplined trading program, and if you are not ready or experienced enough, doubling up or more on your future trades in a desperate attempt to make money back is a bad idea. Rather than help you recover from losses, more times than not this is going to deepen them instead. Another way this can rear its ugly head is buying call options on a stock that keeps dropping. Traders will do this hoping to make up for previous losses, thinking that they are getting the stock at a bargain. Be careful and wait until you see the stock showing solid signs of price movement before you take action like that.

Trading Illiquid Options

Remember in earlier chapters we emphasized that you should only trade options that have an open interest of 100 or more. Trading illiquid options can get you into trouble. Let's say that you are trading a call option on some stock that has less trading interest than the top players. The stock moves up $1, and your in the money option goes up $90 and so you place a sell order. But you've made the mistake of trading an illiquid option, and there are no takers. As you wait for the order to fill, the stock starts dropping. Pretty soon your $90 profit has dropped to $40, and then to $20, until finally your deal closes with a buyer.

So now you've lost all that profit.

If the option is a popular one, with an option interest of 100 or higher, that kind of scenario is not likely to happen. You want to stick with options that are going to trade in an instant, so that you will be able to get in and out of your trades when you need to.

Chapter 5: Understanding The Options Greeks

Every stock option has four metrics associated with it called the "Greeks", because they are denoted by Greek letters. If you are going to trade options you don't need to know the mathematical details of how the Greeks are calculated, but you need to know what the Greeks represent and how to interpret their values.

The Greeks are the underlying factors that will let you determine future options pricing. Keep in mind that when you look up the Greeks, you are seeing a snapshot. The values of the Greeks will change when the underlying fundamental values change.

In all, there are five "Greeks". You can look them up for any option and they are going to be straightforwardly listed under "The Greeks". These are delta, theta, rho, gamma, and vega. In this chapter we will learn what each of these means and how you can use them to make better options trades.

Delta

The first Greek is one of the most important, delta. This Greek gives you an estimate of how the price of an option is going to change in response to the change in the price of the underlying stock. In the image below, we see the Greeks for an Apple call option with a strike price of $215 that expires on 10/18. Here notice that Delta is 0.60.

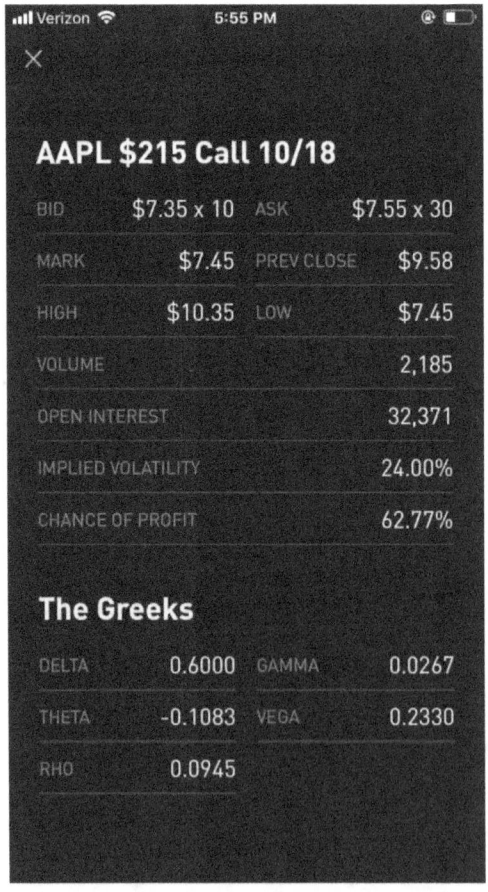

This means that if the stock were to rise or fall by $1, the price of this option would rise or fall by $0.60. Currently the share price is $217.75, and the option price is $7.45. So if the share price rises to $218.10, a gain of $0.35, the option price will rise by 0.60 x $0.35 = $0.21 to $7.66. Remember that this is a per share price, so the actual option price will rise from $745 to $766, a pretty substantial gain.

Something you need to get a feel for is how delta tends to change as time passes for the option. Looking at the $215 call option for Apple, we can compare different dates. It is now Sept. 22, to give you a reference point. Here is delta for the same $215 call for the following expiration dates:

- Sept. 27: 0.6537
- Oct. 4: 0.6072
- Oct. 18: 0.6
- Jan. 17: 0.58
- Jan. 21 (in 2 years): 0.6474

Notice that the LEAP (expiring in 2 years) has a delta that is similar to the option that expires in a week. This makes trading LEAPS valuable, because LEAPS are not nearly as impacted by time decay, but they can gain value by price movements of the underlying stock.

Also notice that the option that expires in a shorter time period has a higher delta than options that expire further out. Ignoring LEAPS, options that expire in a shorter time period have more impact by Delta. The closer to expiration the option gets, the higher delta gets.

Now let's look at the relationship between strike price and delta. So we will stick to one expiration date, and for this discussion we will use the September 27th expiration date for the Apple call options. Here is delta for some different strike prices:

- $225: 0.1544
- $220: 0.3834
- $215: 0.6000
- $200: 0.9488

The share price is $217.75, so the $225 and $220 call options are out of the money, and the $215 and $200 call options are in the money. The more in the money an option is, the higher delta will be. Notice that for the $200 call, delta is practically at 95%. So the more in the money a call option is, the more closely it will track the share price.

As a general rule of thumb, if an option is in the money by 10% of the share price, that means that your delta will be 0.95 or greater. So if you are looking to trade options with a high delta so that you can maximize gains, for a stock with a share price of $100, buy a call option with a strike price of $90 or lower. For a stock with a share price of $200, buy a call option with a share price of $180 or lower, and so on.

Out of the money options are going to be more heavily influenced by time decay, than they are by the share price. This is reflected in the Apple options, where we see that the out of the money option with a strike price that is $2.25 out of the money has a delta of 0.3834, while the option that is $7.25 out of the money has a delta of 0.1544. This is one reason why it's harder to make profits trading out of the money options if they are far out of the money, because for that example if the stock were to rise by $1 you would only gain a little more than 15 cents a share. But, it's also important to recognize that you would still be making profits and the amount of capital you'd have to invest would be smaller. Let's compare the amount of profit you'd make from a $1 move in the stock price to the price paid to buy the option.

First let's take the $200 option. The price is currently quoted at $18.10, and so you would pay $1,810 to buy this option. If the price of the stock goes up $1, you would gain $0.9488 per share, or a total gain of $94.88.

Your ROI would be:

$94.88/$1810 x 100 = 5.24%

Now let's compare this to the $220 option, which has a delta of 0.3834. The $220 call option is only $1.80, so your total investment would only be $180, and a $1 rise in the share price would mean a gain of $38.34.

Your ROI in this case would be:

$38.34/$180 x 100 = 21.3%

This is an important lesson – it shows that you can make money on out of the money options. When you read online articles about this, they dump on the idea and label it a "beginner" mistake. The problem is a lot of people writing online articles about options traders are academics who never actually trade options. Would you be worried about a "beginner mistake" that brought you 21% returns?

You would have to sink $1810 into a single option in order to make the $95 profit. What if you bought 10 $220 options instead? Then you'd make $383.40 on an investment of about the same size.

Keep this in mind when determining what options to trade. Every stock is going to be different, but in the case of Apple at the present time trading in the money options is an expensive proposition – but you can earn money trading out of the money call options and do it even better.

If an option is at the money or close to it, the value of delta is going to be around 0.50.

Now let's take a look at put options. When you see delta for a put option, it's quoted as a negative value. The reason is that the relationship between put options and the price of the underlying stock is an inverse relationship, and so to describe it you need the negative sign. So all that means is if delta is -0.35, the price of the option will increase by $0.35 a share if the price of the stock *drops* by $1. Conversely, if the price of the stock rises by $1, the price of the option will drop by $0.35 a share.

Otherwise, the relationship between delta and the price of the underlying stock works the same way. That is think in terms of expiration date and whether or not the stock options is in the money, out of the money, or at the money. If a put option is out of the money, meaning that the strike price is below the share price, then the delta will be less than -0.50, and the more out of the money the option is, the smaller delta will be.

If the strike price of a put option is higher than the share price, the put option will be in the money. This means that delta will be larger than -0.50 (larger meaning more negative).

Looking at Apple for some specific examples, a $220 put option is slightly in the money, and has a delta of -0.6149. A $225 put option, which is more in the money with a share price of $217.75, has a delta of -0.8356.

Now consider some out of the money examples. The $215 put is slightly out of the money. We find that the delta value for this option is -0.3420. The $210 put has a delta of -0.1666.

Delta as a Probability

Another way to look at delta is it gives you a rough probability estimate that the option will expire in the money. So if you see a call option with a delta of 0.84, this can be basically taken to mean that there is an 84% chance that this option is going to expire in the money. In contrast, if you find an out of the money option that has a delta of 0.38, say, that means there is only a 38% chance that particular option is going to expire in the money.

The same interpretation works for put options, but take the absolute value or just drop the negative sign. If you see a put option with a delta of -0.62, that would mean there is a 62% chance that the option would expire in the money.

If you are going to be looking into selling options rather than just trading options (that is, selling to open options contracts) then this will be an important metric to look at. This is because as a seller of options contracts you actually don't want them to expire in the money, and so you want to sell options that have a relatively low probability of expiring in the money.

Gamma and How Delta Changes

Gamma is a Greek that gets less attention, but Gamma tells you how Delta changes. Every time that either the underlying stock price changes or the days to expiration change, delta will change. The amount that delta will change with future changes in price is estimated by Gamma.

As an example, consider a stock with a share price of $200 and a strike price of $200, with 20 days remaining until expiration. In this case, gamma is going to be 0.04. So that means that if the share price rises by $1, the call option will see delta increase by 0.04. This relationship is approximate, you might see it actually rise by 0.05.

Gamma is the same for call and put options with the same strike price and expiration date. The only difference is that put options will see the opposite relationship, that is if the share price rises by $1, delta will drop by about the value of gamma. If the share price decreases by $1, then the value of delta for a put option will grow larger by about gamma.

If the share price of a stock was $201 with a put option having a strike price of $200, gamma is 0.04 and delta for the put option is − 0.45. So we are going to expect to see delta go to -0.49 or so if the share price of the stock drops by $1. In fact that is exactly what would happen.

The greater the distance between the share price and the strike price, the smaller gamma becomes. This reflects the fact that delta is not going to change as much if there is a larger gap. For in the money options, delta will be approaching 1.0, and so there will be less movement in the value of delta with each change in the share price. Far out of the money options also don't see delta change much in response to changes in the underlying share price.

Now let's keep everything fixed for the moment, and focus on call options for the sake of simplicity. Let's say that the share price is $200 and we have a call option with a strike price of $198. Keeping everything fixed to see how gamma changes, we will consider the values at 30 days, 15 days, 10 days, and 3 days to expiration. At 30 days to expiration, delta is 0.59 and gamma is 0.04.

Now at 15 days to expiration, keeping everything else the same except the time to expiration of the option, delta changes to 0.61, and gamma rises to 0.05. This indicates that the option is becoming more sensitive to changes in the underlying stock price. At 10 days to expiration, delta rises to 0.63, and gamma rises again, this time to 0.06.

Remember that gamma is the same value for a put option that has the same strike price and expiration date.

Now let's move to 3 days to expiration. At this point, delta for the put option rises to 0.72. Gamma rises again as well, this time reaching a value of 0.10.

Delta Values for the Put and the Call

Another interesting observation is that throwing out the negative sign for the delta value for the put option, the sum of delta for the call and for the put for the same strike price and expiration date is 1.0.

Using the previous example, at 3 days to expiration with a share price of $200 and a strike price of $198, delta for the call option is 0.72 and delta for the put option is 0.28. Using the probability, we have an estimate that there is a 72% chance that the call option is going to expire in the money, and there is only a 28% chance that the put option is going to expire in the money. Since they sum to unity, as they must for a probability, you know what the delta value is for the other type of option that has the same strike price and expiration date.

Intrinsic and Extrinsic Value

Options have pricing value that is divided into intrinsic value and extrinsic value. Intrinsic basically means "inside" or internal value, so its value due to the option itself that comes from the underlying asset. An option gets intrinsic value from the price of the underlying stock as well as from the implied volatility, something that we are going to talk about in a little bit. Extrinsic value is "outside" value, and this comes from the time left to expiration.

The less time there is to expiration, the less extrinsic value the option has. The price of the option is found by adding up the extrinsic and intrinsic value. A call option with a strike price of $198 and a share price of $200 with 30 days left until expiration has a price of $542. The extrinsic value of the option is $342, and the intrinsic value of the option is $200. The $200 reflects the difference in the strike price and the share price, which is $2.

If all things remain equal, at 3 days to expiration the intrinsic value is still $200- that is expected because the underlying facts haven't changed as far as the worth of the option which comes from its strike price relative to the share price. At this point, however, extrinsic value has dropped by a large amount. Now the extrinsic value is only

0.60 (per share) giving a total contribution of $60 to the option price of $260. Note that in the money options have intrinsic value but out of the money options have no intrinsic value.

Theta

The third Greek that is of interest is a very important Greek – this is theta. It's important because it is an estimate of time decay. Remember that options lose value as the expiration date approaches because there is less time for the option to move in the money enough to make it worth exercising. This is the true value of the option, whether it's worth exercising to buy or sell the shares. Even if you are trading options only to trade them, keep that in mind.

So what theta is going to tell you, is it will give you the amount of value your option is going to lose at rollover to the next trading day. Theta is quoted as a negative number to reflect the fact that the option is going to decrease in price, and it is given on a per share basis, just like everything else related to options.

So if you see theta quoted as -0.10, that means that at the start of the next trading day, your option will drop in value by 10 cents a share for a total of $10 at market open. You will see this happen if you are following your option at market open, but it is possible that other factors are going to be in play. Let's illustrate this with an example so that we can understand how this works.

Let's return to our example of an option with a $198 strike price, and a share price of $200. We will consider both the call and the put options to see how this works. Theta will be similar for the call and the put options, but it won't be exactly the same. In this case, for the call option theta is -0.12. So that means the option will drop in value by $12 at market open. For the put option, it will drop about the same amount, theta in that case is -0.118.

The call option at our hypothetical market close with 10 days left to expiration is priced at $363, with an extrinsic value of $163. The total price loss will be for the extrinsic value, so at market open the following morning the extrinsic value for this option is going to drop to $151, since theta is -0.12.

The put option has a similar extrinsic value, of $1.62 on a per share basis. So we expect it to drop to $1.50 the next morning. Note that since this put option is out of the money, it has zero intrinsic value.

Rolling over to the following morning, the price of the options drops as expected. The call option drops to $351 for the total price. As expected, the extrinsic value has dropped to $151. Nothing can be done about this – it will keep dropping with each passing day and it doesn't matter what happens to the other factors associated with the option.

But does that mean that the options is a losing bet? Not at all – changing share prices can change the price of the option far more than time decay. In this case, for the call option delta is 0.64f, so for every $1 rise in share price, the price of the option is going to rise by around $64. So if the share price were to rise to $201, the call option would rise in price to $418. We lost $12 in extrinsic value, but the rising share price means that we've had a net gain of $55. The put option drops in price to $117 in this scenario.

Now let's step back and return the share price to $200 to see what happened as a result of time decay to the put option. The price of the put option dropped from $162 to $150 as expected from the theta value. So we see that if the share price rises to $201 after market open, the put option drops even further to the $117 price we noted earlier. But if instead the share price dropped to $198, the put option would actually increase in value by a lot, to $235. That scenario would totally wipe out the value lost due to time decay.

The point of this exercise is to understand that every single day at market open, options lose some value from time decay. However, markets are not static and small changes in share price can more than account for the losses associated with time decay. So it's not necessary to panic when worrying about time decay, or when you see your option drop in value during the first few minutes the market opens. By the end of the day things can be quite different. Time decay only happens once a day at market open.

Vega

Vega is a "Greek" that is related to changes in implied volatility. As you know from looking at any stock market chart, stock prices are "volatile" which basically means that they change a lot. Stock market curves are not smooth, they are jagged as prices swing up and down. This up and down movement is referred to volatility and the more wild the price swings the more volatile the stock.

Volatility is something that has an impact on options prices. Remember what we discussed with time decay. Options have more extrinsic value when there is more time before option expiration because that gives the stock more chances to move, and move in such a way that the option gains in value because for a call option the share price can move higher than the strike price, or for a put option that gives more opportunity for the share price to move lower than the strike price.

More volatility also means more value for an option as well. The more volatility there is, the larger the price swings that the stock is experiencing. And so that means there is an increased probability that the price is going to swing in such a way as to make the option worth more. It might even only be worth more for a short time period, but that is an opportunity to sell and make larger profits.

Implied volatility is a little bit different than volatility. You can look up any stock and get an idea of how it's volatility relates to the market average. This is done by checking *beta*. If beta is equal to 1.0, then the stock has average volatility. If beta is greater than 1.0, then the stock has more volatility than average. A volatility of 1.72 means that the stock is 72% more volatile than the stock market average. If beta is less than 1.0, then the stock is less volatile than the market average.

Volatility is not something that is fixed. It will increase as you get closer to the date of an earnings call, for example. For options, the key concept is implied volatility, which is volatility that is expected in the future. Higher implied volatility can make options prices rise. If volatility is lower, then options prices will drop. As you approach an earnings call, which can send stocks moving aggressively in one direction or another, implied volatility can increase by large amounts causing options prices to increase by large amounts.

If volatility is 19%, then vega will be 0.124. That gives us a rough idea of how the options price will change if the volatility goes up or down by a point. Considering a strike price of $95 for an option on a stock with share price of $100. With 14 days to expiration and a volatility of 14%, a call option will have a price of $504.

Vega is 0.013. A 2 point rise in volatility will cause the option price to rise to $508. If the volatility rose to 20%, the option price would rise to $518. Vega changes as volatility changes, it would rise to 0.032. That indicates that the more volatility rises, the more sensitive the option price is to further changes in volatility.

Volatility doesn't have as much impact on options pricing as changes in the underlying asset price, but near events like earnings calls volatility can rise quite high, making it an important factor. In our example, if volatility rose to 42%, then the option price would jump to $631.

Rho

The final "Greek" is Rho, which is related to interest rates. When interest rates rise, this tends to hurt options prices, but the impact is not that large. Rho gives an estimate of the impact of a 1% rise in interest rates. This is given in terms of the "risk-free rate", which is related to 10 year US Treasuries.

Chapter 6: Options Strategies for Unchanging Prices: The Iron Condor and Iron Butterfly

A lot of the focus in introductory treatments of options is on buying calls or puts to take advantage of rising or falling stock prices. However, these kinds of options trades suffer from one major weakness – having to predict the direction of a price move.

Of course sometimes this is possible within reasonable bounds. You can learn subjects like technical analysis, chart signals, trending, and candlestick charts to make fairly reasonable estimates of price-movements of stock. However this is still fairly risky activity, in the sense that you are just as likely to be wrong as you are to be right in many cases. There are some options traders that do trade straight call options, but most professional options traders do not approach the markets in this way.

That is because while you can strike gold sometimes, it's hard to do it day in and day out. The main weakness in the equation is predicting the direction of a stock price move. But what if we approach options trading in a new and different way, and instead of doing that, remove the directional movements entirely? There are a few different strategies that can be used to do this.

There are also many different situations that occur in the stock market. After an earnings call, the stock can move high or low by large amounts in one direction. As you may know, this usually depends on whether or not earnings "beat" or fail to beat expectations. To be completely honest, this is a bit absurd. If the analysis believe a certain amount of profit is going to be made in a given quarter, but the company makes profit but it's less profit than was projected, this is considered a major "disappointment" and it can cause stock prices to drop by a large amount. If the company happens to beat these imaginary expectations, then stock prices can be sent soaring.

But at other times, the stock is going to be trapped within a range of prices. This can happen for long time periods. The range might be quite constrained, and so it can be hard to make profits by trading calls and puts when the stock is in this pattern. But it turns out that the ability to have calls and puts together enables us to come up with schemes that can earn profits in unexpected ways. We are going to have a look at some of these in this chapter.

The Iron Condor

The first type of trade that we are going to look at is called an iron condor. This is something you want to apply when the highs and lows of stock prices seem to be bounded. It is as if the stock price is trapped. It never breaks above a certain pricing level, called *resistance*. But it never drops below a given price level, which is called the *support*. Sometimes stock can be trapped in this pattern for a long time period. It will look something like this:

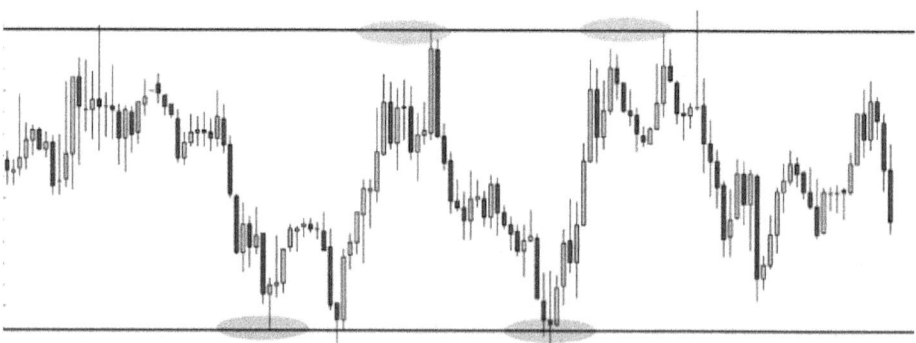

In order to have support and resistance, you want to see the price touch the line of support at least two times, and the line of resistance at least two times. The difference in prices might be relatively small. Of course, there are some possibilities for trading calls and puts, when the price drops down to the support level, you can buy call options and take profit as the price goes back up toward the resistance price level. Then you can buy put options and sell them when the price drops back down to support.

But there is another way to profit from this kind of price trap, as I like to call it. This type of trade is called an iron condor. Among options traders looking to earn an income, the iron condor is one of the most popular ways to trade. If you set it up correctly, it's possible to earn repeated income.

Let's take a minute for an important aside before we show you how to setup the trade. There are two kinds of options traders. One type of options traders is a profit seeking trader. Of course all traders hope to make profits, but a profit seeking trader is one who makes bets on what the stock is going to do, and they roll the dice and gamble hoping to make profits.

The other type of options trader is an income trader. This type of options trader seeks to minimize risk and setup trades so that they can earn regular income from the markets. There are many different ways to do this, and most of them involve *selling* rather than buying options. When you are a regular options trader, you *buy* to open your positions. So you are going to be running your business buying low, and selling high in order to make profits.

An income trader sells to open their positions. They seek to make money selling options and while you have been concerned about things like theta and time decay so far, as an income trader you actually value time decay and can't wait for options to expire.

An iron condor is the first type of strategy that we are going to consider that works in this fashion. When you trade an iron condor, you are going to sell it to open your position. Then you are going to make money from the time decay. As long as the stock stays within the range that you use to define the iron condor, you will earn a profit. If it moves outside the range of the iron condor, then you are going to lose money.

So let's see how its setup. The idea of an iron condor is to set boundaries on the stock price, so we are going to be looking for a ranging stock price as shown in the graph above. To set upper bounds, we are going to use call options. The lower bounds of the range are going to be set by using put options.

A single iron condor isn't going to make you a huge amount of money. The basic philosophy behind it is that this is a limited risk − limited profit type of trade. It eliminates having to guess which direction the stock is going to move, and instead we are only going to estimate the bounds of stock price movement over the lifetime of the option. Under normal conditions this type of bet is going to work in most cases. Of course, if there is unexpected news, such as bad news coming out about the company, that can cause prices to move outside the bounds of the iron condor and turn the trade into a loser. Unexpectedly bad news about the economy or political situation can have the same effect.

Let's also talk about volatility. If you recall from the last chapter, when volatility is high that means stock prices are swinging between high highs and low lows. Since we are looking for a situation where stock prices are basically bounded in a narrow range of prices, that means that an iron condor is a type of trade you want to use when volatility is relatively low.

To create an iron condor, we are going to trade 4 options at once. We are going to sell two options and buy two options. First let's look at the high price range for the trade. First, we want to sell a call option with a lower strike price. The strike price used for the call option sets the upper boundary of the iron condor. So you are setting this up with the belief that the stock price is not going to exceed the strike price of the call option that you select.

Second, we are going to buy a call option that has a higher strike price than the first call option. This is done because we are going to use it to hedge our risks a little bit. Let's see how that would work. For our example, we will assume that the stock price is $200.

We could sell a call option with a strike price of $205. This means we are setting up our iron condor with the belief that from now until the expiration date of the option, the price of the stock is not going to rise above $205. If there are 30 days to expiration, and volatility is a relatively low 15%, the price of a call option with a $205 strike price is going to be $1.55.

The breakeven price is found by adding the cost of the call option to the strike price, which would give $206.55. As long as the share price stays at $206.55 or below, it's not worth it for the option to be exercised. However, if the share price goes above that value, the option can be exercised. In the case of a call option, as the options seller, this means that you have to sell 100 shares of stock at the strike price of $205 a share.

So how would that work in practice? The way it actually works is your broker buys the shares at the market price, sells the shares to the counterparty to the option contract to close the transaction at the lower strike price, and then they stick you with the losses. So if the share price was $208, you would have a $3 loss per share, or a total loss of $300 for each contract that would cover 100 shares of stock.

Of course stock prices can rise to any value, at least in theory. So you could be getting into real trouble if the stock price rose much higher. The iron condor caps maximum losses by including a second call option, with a higher strike price. You buy this call option, which means you cap possible profits because you have this added expense. But besides limiting possible profits, it will also cap possible losses.

Since you are buying a call option, you can exercise your rights on that option and buy shares of stock at that strike price that you can sell at the higher market price to make up for some of the loss.

Using our price setup, we could choose $210 as the second strike price. Suppose that the stock price rises to $212. In this situation, the first option with the $205 strike price is going to be exercised. So we have to buy shares at $212 and then sell them to the counterparty of the $205 option at $205 a share, giving us a net loss of $7 a share.

But now we can exercise the second call option that we have purchased. In this case, we buy shares of stock at $210, but then we sell them on the market for $212, giving us a net $2 a share. This helps mitigate the total losses, reducing the total loss to $5 a share, or a total loss of $500. The loss is capped. It's going to be the difference between the two strike prices chosen for our options.

Now let's turn our attention to the other side of the trade. This time, we will have two put options. First we set the lower boundary for the iron condor by selling a put option. We can make it any value we want, but to have a nice symmetrical iron condor we will choose a strike price of $195. Generally speaking, a ten dollar range is a very good one to have for an iron condor. The probability of the stock price going outside a range of ten dollars is relatively low, assuming you have correctly picked a low volatility situation.

The options that you sell are the ones that set the boundaries for the iron condor. In this case, we have the call option with a strike price at $205, and a put option with a strike price of $195. That means as long as the stock price stays in between $195 and $205 between the time we sell to open this position and when the options expire, we will earn a profit.

In addition to selling a put option, we will attempt to mitigate risk in the same way that we did with our setup of the call options. This means that we are going to buy a put option with a lower strike price in order to set the final lower boundary for the iron condor. Again, it can be any value, but for the sake of clarity we will put it at the same $5 distance.

Now let's take a look at what would happen if the stock price went outside the range we have setup to the downside. We have sold a put option with a strike price of $195, and purchased a put option with a strike price of $190. If the share price of the stock falls below $195 but remains above $190, the put option that we sold is can be exercised. When a put option is exercised that means that we will be forced to buy shares of stock at the strike price. So, we have to buy shares at $195 a share even though the price on the market is between $190 and $195, let's say for the sake of example it's $192. We then have to sell the shares at the market price. So if we sell the shares for $192, we are out $3 a share for a total loss of $3 a share.

If the stock price kept dropping, we would find ourselves with ever increasing losses. But that is why we buy the second put option, it serves the same purpose as the second call option in mitigating our losses. So if the share price drops to say $170, our losses will be capped at the difference between the strike prices of the two put options. Instead of being forced to sell the shares at the market price of $170 a share, we would be able to exercise the second put option and sell the shares at $190 a share. So we had to buy them at $195 a share even though the market price was $170 a share, but then we are able to sell them to someone else for $190 a share.

I've actually simplified the discussion a little bit, because you have to incorporate the net costs of entering the positions. Since you get a credit for entering an iron condor – you sell it to open – this actually mitigates your risk even further. Let's see what the prices are for each of the options in this case:

- $210 Call Option (BUY): $0.57

- $205 Call Option (SELL): $1.55
- $195 Put Option (SELL): $1.45
- $190 Put Option (BUY): $0.47

The cost of buying the two options is $0.57 + $0.47 = $1.04. But, we receive a credit from selling the other two options of $1.55 + $1.45 = $3. Our net credit is $3-$1.04 = $1.96.

We start out ahead by $1.96. So if we end up losing on the trade because the stock breaks one way or another, our losses which were already capped at $5 are actually reduced by this amount, and so our total possible loss in any situation is $5 - $1.96 = $3.04. That means the maximum possible loss is $304 (for the total of 100 shares) and the maximum profit, which is fixed, is $196. This type of situation is shown in an iron condor graph:

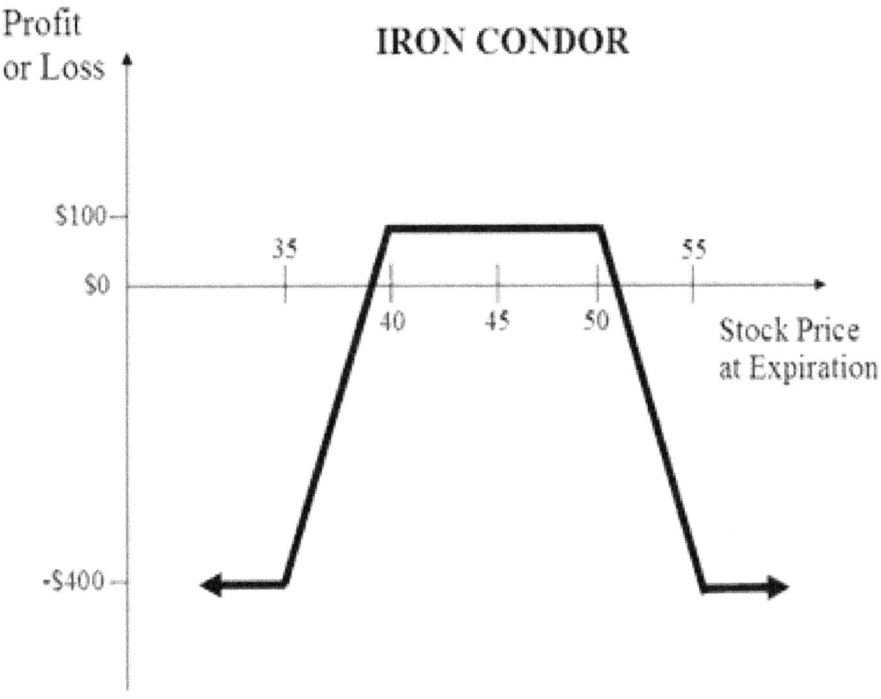

The above example shows an iron condor with inner strike prices of $40 and $50 for a lower priced stock, with a max profit of $100 and max loss of $400.

In the two examples we've discussed so far, the losses seem to outstrip the gains. However, that is a deceiving way to look at the trade. With an iron condor, the probability of winning on the trade – provided that you've done your homework and picked a stock in a low volatility situation, means that your probability of winning on the trade is high.

The key to succeeding with an iron condor is carefully studying and choosing your trades. Don't just randomly pick a stock and then enter an iron condor.

If the iron condor stays within the range you setup, the options are going to be losing value from time decay as the days pass because all of the options are going to be out of the money. For this reason iron condor traders often say they are making money from time decay.

Buying Back to Close

One strategy people use is they buy back the iron condor to close the position. You can chose to do this or not. The reason you would do it would be if there is a possibility of the stock breaking one way or the other, and then you would be put in a position of having the options that you sold exercised. That means that the counterparty to the transaction would choose to buy or sell the shares of stock. When you sell an option and it's exercised, we say that you have been assigned.

When you are assigned you have an obligation to carry out the terms of the contract, however this all happens automatically in these types of options trades. The broker is going to take care of this for you and so you aren't even going to know what is happening other than seeing the losses that show up in your account.

You can trade iron condors on different time frames. The longer you select for your time frame, the longer you are going to have to wait for either time decay to work well enough for you to buy it back and still make a profit, or for you to let it expire and make the maximum profit.

If you decide to buy it back early, then you can still make a profit but it will be a smaller profit than you could have made. The closer to the expiration date the better. If the stock price is staying within the range, and there isn't any indication that it's going to breakout one way or the other, then it is generally pretty safe to simply let the iron condor expire. Many traders like to play it safe and buy it back with a few days left. At that point, the time decay has whittled down the prices of the options, so buying them back is not going to eat into your profits too much.

Assignment can happen at any time, but its most likely going to happen when the options expire. Many people get misled by statements such as "most options expire worthless". Here is a fact – if you have in the money options that you have sold, and they are allowed to expire – they are going to be exercised. All in the money options that expire are exercised automatically by the broker. In the case of a trade like an iron condor, losses are mitigated. So hopefully you have enough funds in your account to cover any losses.

If you are close to expiration and there is a breakout one way or the other, rather than letting the contracts expire, buy them back. You are going to take losses in that case, but it's better to take limited losses than it is to let the options expire and then get stuck with an even worse situation. The point is buying them back early is more than likely going to mean buying them back, taking some losses, but avoid having the options exercised.

Iron Condor: Summary

So an iron condor is a type of trade that you want to get into when you believe that the underlying stock is not going to see much price movement between the time that you open the position and the expiration date of the options. Although we've talked about each of the four options that are involved in setting up an iron condor as if these are separate trades, you enter an iron condor in a single trade. All four options will have the same expiration date, but they will have different strike prices as described. You can setup an iron condor for any time frame that you like, but most professional traders tend to go for a 30 or 45 day time frame prior to expiration.

Maximum profit for the iron condor is given by the net credit your receive when opening the position. So it's the sum of the payments you receive for selling the two options with the inner strike prices, minus the amount you pay to buy options with the outer strike prices. The inner strikes set the price boundaries for the iron condor. You have losses if the share price goes outside the boundaries set by the inner strikes at expiration.

Possible losses have to be calculated at both sides of the trade. In our example, we setup an iron condor that was symmetric and so possible losses were the same. For each side of the trade, the maximum possible loss is the difference between the outer strike price and the inner strike price, minus your net credit for selling the iron condor.

There are tradeoffs to be made in setting up iron condors. You can increase the probability of profit, but this will decrease the amount of possible profit you can make. Taking more risk means you can earn more profit. A higher risk scenario means that the range setup by the inner strikes is narrower. However, you can increase your profit margins by selecting wider ranges between the inner and outer strike prices. But that means if the trade turns out to be a losing trade, you can end up losing higher amounts of money.

In most cases, iron condors are going to have possible losses that are larger than maximum possible profit. But the loss is capped, and then probability of profit is higher. The strategy used by most iron condor traders is to enter trades with smaller profits, and higher probability of profit and then make up for it by entering into a larger number of trades. If you are making $200 per trade and want to make

$5,000 a month trading iron condors, then you simply enter into 25 trades a month.

You can do multiple instances of a given trade if you think it has a high probability of success, but you should also use some diversification in your trading strategy. Just like trading calls and puts, trading iron condors is going to have some risk of failure, and you are going to be losing on some of the trades.

Iron Butterfly

An iron butterfly is a different type of trade that also involves four options. This time, you are hoping to hit a specific share price to maximize profits, but the trade can also be setup with a directional bias one way or the other. In the case of an iron butterfly, we modify the iron condor by selling put and call options at the same strike price.

For the iron condor example, we sold a call and put option at inner strike prices of $205 and $195, respectively. Then we bought a call and put option with outer strike prices at $210 and $190 respectively. The setup made a profit if the stock stayed in between the inner strike prices, that is within the range of $195-205.

In the case of an iron butterfly, we would set up the trade as follows. We would sell a call option with a strike price of $200, and also sell a put option with a strike price of $200, and both with the same expiration date. Then we would set up a range by buying a put option at $195 and buying a call option with a strike price of $205.

The hope with the iron butterfly is that the stock price stays at or close to $200. This will give us the maximum profits. We can close out the position early if necessary just like with the iron butterfly.

The net credit received for an iron butterfly are the premiums you receive for selling the call and put at the center strike price, minus the premiums paid for buying the outer call and put options.

The maximum loss is going to be the larger of either: the difference between the middle strike price and the lower strike price less the credit received, or the difference between the upper strike price and the middle strike price less the credit received.

In our example, we made it symmetrical and so we can take the middle strike price minus the strike price of the purchased put option, or $200-$195 = $5, and then subtract the net credit received. For the case of a $200 strike price, we would receive a credit of $6.87 per share. The $195 put would cost $1.45, and the $205 call would cost $1.55, so the net credit is ($6.87 - $1.45 - $1.55) x 100 = $387. That would be the maximum possible profit if the share price stayed close to $200.

A graph of an iron butterfly from the options guide on Wikipedia is shown below.

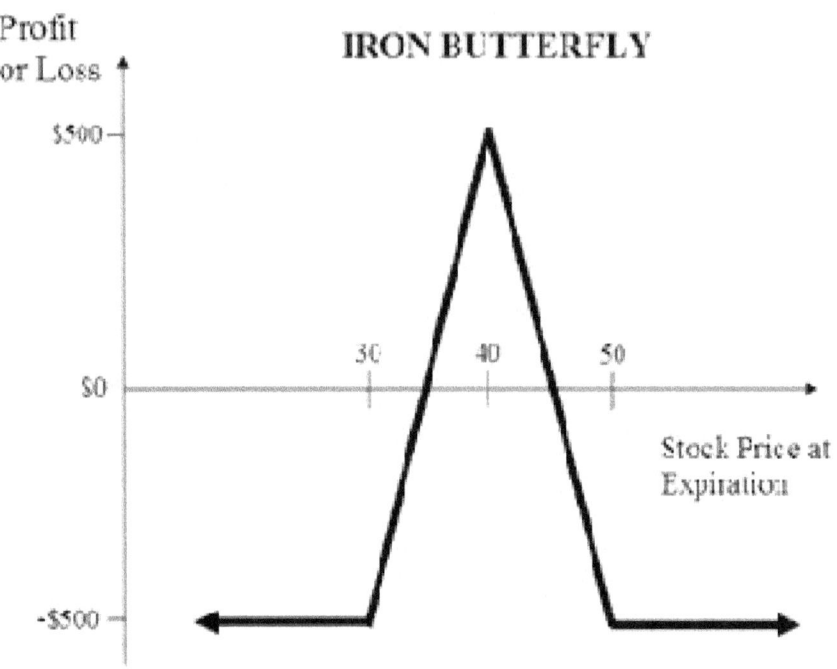

Summary: Profits From Stock Not Moving

The iron condor is a more popular trading strategy, because the iron butterfly relies on the stock staying basically at the same price, while the iron condor gives the stock a range that it can move about in. An iron condor is a good strategy that can be used to generate regular income. Many traders only trade using iron condors, but you can also mix up iron condor trading with other strategies in order to produce a level of income that you want.

Chapter 7: Trading Breakout Prices Using Strangles and Straddles

In the last chapter, we considered the case of stock prices staying within a certain range. Now we are going to consider the opposite situation, and that would be a stock price breaking out. The stock price can break out to the upside or the downside, it doesn't matter. That is the beauty of options strategies, we can take advantage of price movements without knowing or having to estimate which direction the prices are going to go.

There are two main strategies that are used for this purpose. They are called strangle and straddle. The setups are a little bit different but they accomplish the same purpose. Strangles are more popular.

Before setting up a trade like this, think about the reasons that you would do so. When we setup this type of trade, the reality is that the trade can make a profit from a price movement of increasing stock prices, or a price movement of decreasing prices. So the direction of the price movement is not relevant. The price movement does have to be relatively large, so we are looking for a breakout price movement.

This would indicate that some important news or event is going to be the time to apply this strategy. In fact, there are four times a year you can apply this type of strategy on any stock. That would be when quarterly earnings are reported. Strong breaks in prices are very common after earnings calls. The beauty of these strategies is that we know there are going to be large movements in stock prices after the earnings calls of companies that are popular to trade, however we don't care which direction the stock moves. New productions, product, or service announcements can also lead to large price movements in a stock.

You can also apply these strategies on index funds, which will change dramatically in response to events like interest rate changes, GDP growth announcements, jobs reports, and international or political events. DIA and SPY are two index funds you can use with these strategies.

Strangles and straddles are debits, that is you buy to open these positions and then sell them to close out your position, hopefully at a profit.

Strangle

A strangle is set up by using a call and a put option in order to set a bounded range of stock prices. But unlike the iron condor, the goal in this case is to earn profits when the stock price moves outside the boundary that we have created, rather than profiting when the stock price stays inside of it. As the graph below indicates, we will earn a profit when the stock prices are outside the two boundaries set by a call and a put option. It is less complicated than an iron condor because we will simply buy two options to set up the trade.

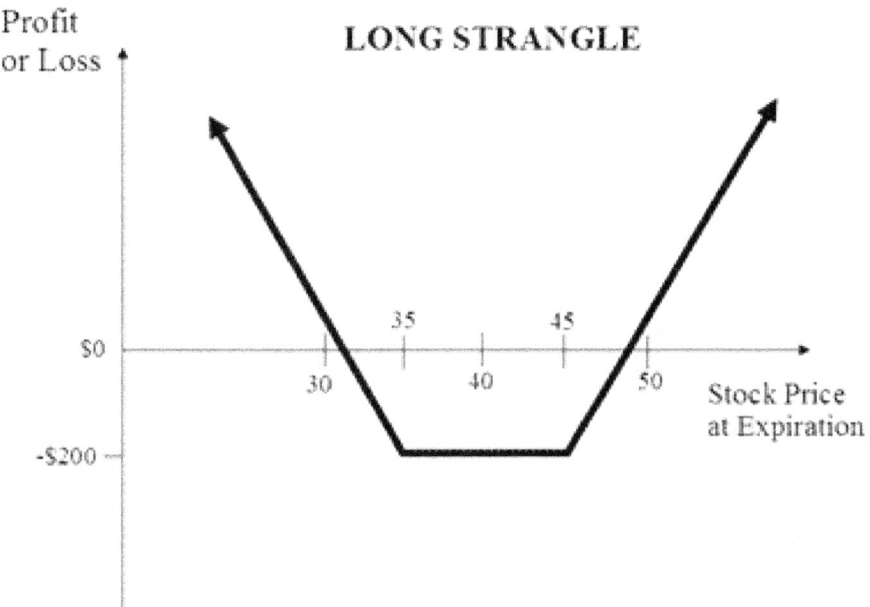

LONG STRANGLE

The goal here is to earn a profit from a large change in share price that can move either up or down. You buy a call option at one strike price, which forms the upper boundary for the trade. Then you buy a put option at a lower strike price but with the same expiration date, that sets up the lower boundary for the trade.

The profit potential for a strangle is quite large. In theory, the profit potential on the upside is unlimited. Of course in the real world stock prices don't increase without limit. We will look at a specific example to get a handle on potential profits.

So if the stock price breaks to the upside, the put option will expire worthless. You are out the price paid for the put option. If the stock breaks to the downside, then the call option will expire worthless.

The setup has two breakeven points, on each side of the trade. On the upside, the breakeven price is the strike price of the call option plus the total premium paid to buy the two options. On the downside, the breakeven points is the strike price of the put option minus the total premium paid to buy the two options.

So let's say that we have a stock trading at $200 a share, and we are going to setup a strangle before an earnings call. We can buy a call option with a strike price of $202 for $210. We can buy a put option with the same expiration date with a strike price of $198 for $205. So our total cost is $415 to enter the trade.

The breakeven price on the downside is $198 - $2.05 = $195.95. So if the stock price drops, it has to drop at least to $195.95 before we can make a profit. On the upside the breakeven price is $202 + $2.10 = $204.10, and so the stock price has to rise at least to $204.10 before we can start making a profit.

We are assuming that we buy these options 14 days to expiration. Let's say that there is an earnings call in 7 days, and so the price action is going to take place with 6 days to expiration. We will assume that the stock price didn't move very much in the interim.

At 6 days to expiration, if there are no other changes the put option is now valued at $109, and the call option is valued at $1.12. So they have lost quite a bit of value. However, before earnings calls implied volatility tends to go up a lot. So for our exercise, we will assume that implied volatility spikes to 45% before the earnings call. Under these conditions, the call option is now priced at $370, and the put option is priced at $364. That gives us a total of $734. Just based on the volatility we could sell at a profit.

Now let's say the earnings call has some surprises and beats expectations. For a $200 a share stock, a rise in price of $10, $20 or more is not unusual. Let's say that it rises $20 a share overnight. That causes the put option to drop to $16 in value, so its worthless. The call option spikes to $1,810. We can sell it at a massive profit, found by subtracting the cost of entering the trade:

$1810 - $415 = $1,395

Now let's say that instead the earnings call has a lot of bad news, and the stock plummets to $170 a share the following morning. In that case, the put option increases in price to $2,800. This time we make a profit of:

$2800 - $415 = $2,385

So we see from this example that we are able to profit with stock moves in either direction.

What if the stock stays in the range? In that case we will lose money on the trade. The maximum loss incurred will be the price paid to buy the options. If the share price stays in between the two strike prices, both options will expire worthless.

Straddle

Now we will consider a similar trade that is called a straddle. A straddle is also designed to earn profits from a breakouts to one side or the other. In the case of a straddle, we will buy a call option and a put option, just like we would do with a strangle. In this case, however, we will have the same strike price for both and the same expiration date.

The goal of a straddle is the same, we hope to profit from large price moves, and it doesn't matter which direction the price goes, up or down is fine. If the price moves to the upside, in theory the maximum profit is unlimited. In reality it is going to be a finite value, minus the total cost required to buy both options to enter the position. Like a strangle, this is a net debit, and so you buy to open this position.

To the downside, in theory the stock could lose all of its value, but of course that is a very rare event. But you can still make large profits from significant drops in stock prices, such as after an earnings call.

To the upside, the breakeven price is the strike price plus the total premium paid in order to enter the position. So the stock price has to rise at least this amount in order to start earning profits. On the downside, the breakeven price is the strike price less the total price paid to enter the position. So if the stock price drops, it has to drop at least by this amount before we start earning profits.

The maximum possible loss would occur if the share price stayed equal to the strike price used. On a graph of profits and losses, the straddle forms a V shape, with the bottom representing the maximum loss at the strike price.

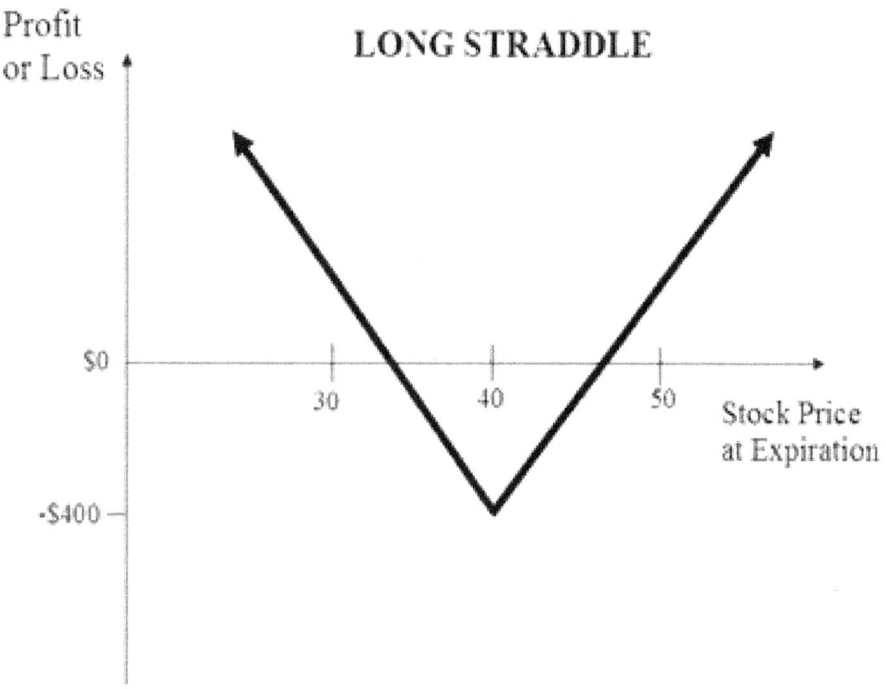

Profit or Loss

LONG STRADDLE

$0

30   40   50

Stock Price at Expiration

-$400

Let's say that we are trading Facebook stock at $186 a share. We buy a call and put option with the at the money $186 strike price with 10 days to expiration. With a high level of volatility, say approaching an earnings call, the prices of each option would be about $429, so the total cost to enter the position would be $858.

Now say with 5 days left to expiration, Facebook announces their earnings. If the earnings call was great news, the stock price could go up, say $15 a share. In that case, the put option expires worthless and the call option rises to $1532 in value, and we earn a profit of:

$1532-$858 = $674

If instead, the news was bad, and the stock dropped $20 a share, the call option would expire worthless and the put option would be priced at $2004. Our total profit would be:

$2004 - $858 = $1,146

Summary: Strangles and Straddles

Strangles and straddles are buy to open positions. You enter into a strangle or a straddle whenever you believe the stock price is going to have a large move in one direction or the other, but you are not sure which direction the stock is going to move. This position enables you to avoid having to predict the direction of the movement of the stock. If things work out as you thought, with a large break in price to the upside or the downside, then one of the options will expire worthless, however the other option will increase dramatically in price allowing you to earn significant profits on the trade.

Chapter 8: Debit and Credit Spreads

The next options strategies that we are going to look at involve unidirectional trading again. The first strategies that we are going to examine are called debit spreads. You can form a debit spread using either a pair of calls, which you would use if you are hoping to see the stock rise in price, or a pair of puts, used when you expect the stock to drop. These essentially serve the same purpose as trading calls and puts, however they provide mitigated risk strategies.

Next, we will look at credit spreads. Credit spreads are a completely different way of trading, with a purpose of generating income rather than looking for the stock to move in a certain way. You can use put credit spreads if it is expected that the stock will stay above a certain value, or you can use call credit spreads if the stock is expected to stay below a certain value.

Call Debit Spreads

The first strategy we will consider is a call debit spread. In this case you are going to buy a call option and also sell a call option at the same time. They will have the same expiration dates, but different strike prices. Since one strike price is higher than another, this is known as a type of vertical spread, the vertical referring to the different strike prices.

A call option with a price that is closer to the stock price is worth more money, and you are going to buy this option. You are hoping to earn a profit from the lower strike price.

So you would enter a call debit spread for the same reasons that you would buy a call option – you are expecting the stock price to increase before the options expire. The purpose of the call with the higher strike price is to mitigate losses. You will sell that call option.

Selling a call option with a higher strike price will lower the cost required to enter the position. This creates a tradeoff, however, because it will reduce the amount of profit that you can make. Like an iron condor, a call debit spread is a limited risk, and limited reward strategy. The probability of earning a profit is increased and your total risk is limited, but your profits are also capped, unlike with simply trading call options which at least in theory have unlimited profit potential.

The maximum profit you can earn on a call debit spread is found by taking the difference between the two strike prices, and then subtracting the premium paid to enter the position. Maximum profit is attained with a call debit spread if the stock price rises to or above the higher strike price. The difference between this type of trade and simply buying a call is that no matter how high the share price rises above the higher strike price, your profit is fixed.

The maximum loss is the net premium paid to enter the position. Let's look at some specific numbers to get a better handle on the call debit spread.

Let's say some stock is trading at $80 a share. We will create a call debit spread by buying a call option with a strike price of $80 and selling a call option with a strike price of $84. We will assume that there are 15 days to expiration.

The call with the $80 strike price is going to cost $123. We sell the call with the $84 strike price, and that brings us a $16 credit, lowering the cost to enter the position to $107. So the maximum profit on a per share basis is:

Difference in strikes – net cost to enter position = $4 - $1.07 = $2.93

Or for 100 shares, our profit will be $293.

The breakeven price for a call debit spread is the strike price of the call we purchase plus the net premium paid. In this case, that would be $80 + $1.07 = $81.07. Profits will gradually increase until we arrive at the $84 strike price, where we get the maximum profit. The maximum profit remains fixed for any higher share price.

Put Debit Spread

If you believe that instead of increasing the stock price is going to drop, but you want to mitigate the potential losses from investing in put options, you can invest using a put debit spread. This works in a similar manner to a call debit spread, but with everything adjusted to the situation of put options.

A put debit spread involves simultaneously buying and selling a put option. We will buy a put option with a given strike price, and then sell a put option with a lower strike price.

The maximum loss that can occur with this trade is the net premium paid, which is the price paid for the higher strike price put less the premium received as a credit for selling the lower strike price put option.

The breakeven point is the higher strike price less the net premium paid.

So if we have a stock trading at $100 a share, and we expect the share price to drop, we can buy a put option with a $100 strike price and sell a put option with a $95 strike price. A put option with a $100 strike price will cost $1.25. A put option with a $95 strike price will net a premium of $0.07, so the total cost to enter the position is $1.18.

The maximum profit is the difference in the strike prices minus the total cost to enter the position, which would be $5 - $1.18 = $3.82.

You can see from these examples that choosing strike prices that are spread out increases the maximum profit that can be made, but at the expense of reducing the mitigation in risk that selling the second option provides.

Put Credit Spreads

In this section we are going to completely change gears. Now we are going to talk about options trading strategies that are designed for the purposes of earning income. Income generating strategies that involve puts and calls without using something like an iron condor can be spreads or they can be traded "naked". We will be looking at the latter case in the next chapter. In this section we are going to be looking at selling put credit spreads.

When selling a put credit spread, you don't really care what the stock is doing as long as it doesn't drop to the level of your strike prices. And so you are looking to sell out of the money put options, and then mitigate your risk by purchasing a put option. This will help limit your losses in the event that the option that you sold is exercised, and the stock price has also dropped below the second strike price.

The way to setup a put credit spread is to sell a put option at a relatively high strike price. However, the strike price should be such that the put option is out of the money. You don't want to sell an in the money put option – because the put option will be exercised when it expires and you'd have to buy the stock. We are setting up this kind of trade hoping that the option is not going to be exercised.

This is an income generating trade, and so we are going to receive a credit to our account for entering the trade. Then after this, we hope that the price just moves along such that the options expire worthless. So we will hope that the strike price stays above the strike price used for the put option that we sell, but other than that we really don't care what the stock does.

The closer the strike price of a put option is to the market price of the stock, the more it is going to be worth. But that also increases the probability that the option can expire in the money, so some care needs to be used. Many successful traders actually trade put options that are far outside the money, at least a standard deviation. This significantly reduces the probability that they are going to expire in the money. But the downside to that is that you will make less money per trade, and to make an income you would then need to enter into a large number of trades.

The maximum profit earned on a put credit spread is the net premium you receive for entering the position. This is a sell to open position, and you will receive a net credit that is given by the premium received for the higher strike price less the premium paid for the lower strike price.

The maximum loss on the trade is figured from buying and selling shares when the options are exercised. Maximum loss is going to occur when the share price drops below the lower strike price.

Even though you receive a credit for entering into this position, you have to put collateral into your account in order to make the trade. The collateral is enough cash so that you could cover the maximum loss should it occur. Let's look at a couple of real world examples.

Google is trading at $1,229.93 a share. We can setup a put credit spread by selling a put option with a strike price of $1232.50, and buying a put option with a strike price of $1,222.50. The two put options used in a put credit spread will have the same expiration dates. Selling a put option is how you make money on this trade, and you buy the other put option to limit the maximum possible loss, should the stock price drop unexpectedly.

This is another limited-risk, limited-reward type strategy. This strategy has fixed profits and losses when entering the trade.

In the case of Google, the $1232.50 put option is selling at $12.60. So we sell this and receive the premium. The $1222.50 put option is $7.60. The profit that we make on this trade is equal to the difference in prices required to enter the trade, $12.60-$7.60 = $5. So we would earn $500 from this spread, if the share price was at or above the upper strike price at expiration.

Now let's look at possible losses. Suppose that the share price stays below the upper strike price. The breakeven point is the upper strike price minus the premium paid. We are actually thinking of the breakeven price for the buyer, because we want to see at what point they would exercise the option. With a high price like this, $12.50 to buy the put option, the breakeven price is $1232.50 - $12.50 = $1220. So the stock has to drop all the way to $1220 before its even worth exercising the option.

But let's say the share price drops low enough so that we hit maximum losses. This occurs when the share price drops below the lower strike price, to say $1210 a share. In that case, the put option we sold will be exercised, meaning that we have to buy shares of stock at the higher strike price of $1232.50. That is a bad scenario for sure, but we can now sell them at the strike price for the other put option, which we had purchased in order to mitigate risks.

Therefore we sell the shares at $1222.50. So right now, we are at a loss of $10 a share, but we received a net credit of $5 a share. Subtracting this from our loss, the total loss on the trade is limited to $5 a share, or $500 in total.

In many cases, it might be more likely that the option gets exercised. If the share price is in between the two strike prices your losses will be lower than if the share price drops below the lower strike price. The function of the lower strike price is to put a cap on the possible losses.

In order to enter into the trade, you would have to make sure that there was enough money in your account to cover possible losses. So in this case, we'd need to have about $500 in our account to act as insurance.

Assuming that you are picking good trades, most of the time you are not going to experience losses on them. So you can use your collateral over and over again when making trades. In this case, you could do weekly repeats of the same trade. Most traders pick around 3-4 stocks that they want to focus on. This approach allows you to get to know the company really well, and so you will be able to have an idea of how the stock moves and make good choices for your strike prices. You could then trade Google every single week, selling put credit spreads that expire every Friday. Using this method you could cobble together a pretty high six figure income using collateral of a few thousand dollars.

Call Credit Spreads

There is another approach which is to use call credit spreads. Under most market conditions, traders prefer to use put credit spreads. But in a bear market, call credit spreads may be more appropriate. With a call credit spread, you are expecting the stock to stay the same or drop in value.

With a call credit spread, you are going to sell a call option with a lower strike price, and buy a call option with a higher strike price. To be successful, you are going to sell your call option that is out of the money, and you are going to hope that the call option will stay out of the money.

If a stock is trading at $200 a share, we could sell a call option with a strike price of $202 with 30 days to expiration for $346. Then we could buy a call option with a strike price of $210 for $114. So when you have a call credit spread, you sell an option with a lower strike price that is out of the money, and then you buy a call option with a higher strike price that is also out of the money.

The profit is fixed, and is equal to the net credit received. For a call option with a lower strike price, you will receive more money than you will pay for a call option with a higher strike price.

The call option that you buy will help you mitigate the risk if the share price rises. Maximum losses will occur if the share price rises above the higher strike price. In that case, you will be assigned and have to sell shares of stock at the lower strike price, but then you can buy share of stock at the higher strike price, and then sell them on the market to recoup some of your losses. The maximum loss is going to be equal to the difference in the strike prices minus the net credit received.

Buying Back to Close

If you sell put or call credit spreads, buying back to close is always a viable strategy to avoid assignment. You want to wait until it is close to expiration. Most options that are exercised are not exercised until they expire, so you can buy back to close and avoid assignment either if the trade has gone bad, meaning that the share price moved in a way against the trade, or you're fearful of a dramatic move of the share price on expiration day. In the event that you are not concerned about price movements of the stock and your options are out of the money as expiration day approaches, you can let the options expire worthless and in that case you will receive the maximum possible profit on the trade.

Chapter 9: Selling Options

In the previous chapter, and also in the chapter on the iron condor, we explored selling options strategies. These were complicated setups that involve trading multiple options in a single trade, and it can involve buying and selling options simultaneously. Selling individual options is a simpler strategy that can be used, but there are some caveats.

The first way of selling options that we are going to look at are covered options. That is, you cover the trade by either having shares of stock on hand or by having enough cash available to buy 100 shares of stock.

The second way of selling options is so-called "naked" selling. In this case you can sell call and put options that are not backed by anything (but in fact you will need to deposit some cash that will function as collateral).

Naked selling is actually the easiest way to earn money as an options trader that is selling premium for income. However, you are required to open a margin account in order to do naked selling, and you have to deposit at least

$2,000 cash in order to do this. To sell enough options to make a good living, you will probably need to put more cash than that. The amount of money required is far less than you would need to actually cover buying shares of stock, but it is still a non-trivial amount of money if you are looking to make a six figure income selling options premium.

Covered Calls

The simplest method of options selling that is known is the covered call. Remember that with a call option, the buyer has the right to buy 100 shares of stock at the strike price. So when you are selling a call option, you have to provide the buyer with those 100 shares of stock if they exercise their rights under the option. In the case of a covered call, you already own the 100 shares of stock, and you are selling call options against the stock that you own.

If you already own shares of stock, this can be a way to generate income. You can sell call options on a monthly or even weekly basis, and pocket the income if you are managing to sell the options with out of the money strike prices, that remain out of the money. Keep in mind that the breakeven price is what matters, and so if you are selling options with a $100 strike price that cost $2, the share price must rise above $102 before anyone is going to exercise the option.

The idea is to be able to repeatedly sell call options against the stock so that you can generate an income from your activities.

In the event that the share price does move high, you can try buying the call options back before expiration. With American style options, they can be exercised on or before the expiration date, so in theory your options could be exercised at any time when the share price moves to breakeven price or higher. The higher the price goes, the more incentive a buyer has to buy the shares of stock. However, studies show that in most cases options are not exercised until expiration. That gives you an opportunity to get out of the trade and hold onto your shares of stock, so that you can sell better call options against them the following week.

If things are going well, you can use the same strategy that is used with credit spreads.

Some traders will buy the options back to close the trade just in case there is a dramatic move of the stock on expiration day. In that case, the options will be cheap (assuming that they are still out of the money) because they have lost their extrinsic value. However, if you feel like there is little risk of a dramatic move in share price, you can hold onto the options contracts so that you will earn maximum possible profits.

Protected Puts

A protected put is a put option you sell while putting enough funds in your account in order to cover buying the shares of stock at the strike price should the option be exercised. A protected put is not a great strategy. In the case of covered calls, we are assuming it's a viable strategy because you are someone who already owns the shares of stock. In that case, you might as well leverage that stock in order to make some income.

But in the case of protected puts, it's not clear that this would be the best possible use of your funds if you have that much money available. Putting up enough money to buy 100 shares of stock can be a substantial sum if we are talking about stocks that have decent share prices. With that much money, you could buy many options, buy shares of stock or use the money for collateral to enter into probably several more trades selling naked puts. The protected put is not a strategy that makes very much sense.

Selling Naked Put Options

Selling naked put options is the most popular income generating strategy that is used in options trading. It turns out that there is a great deal of misinformation about naked put selling. Many financial advisors claim that naked put selling is very risky. In fact it's a pretty simple trading strategy.

It is related to the put credit spread, so you can think of a put credit spread as a risk managed version of this strategy. In the case of a put credit spread, we sold a put option for profit, and then purchased a put option to mitigate possible risk in the case of assignment.

In the case of a naked put option, you are eliminating the purchase of a put option, and you are only going to sell one put option. It really isn't risky, because you can buy the contract back at any time to close the trade.

You begin selling your naked put options by carefully choosing a put option that is far outside the money. Many traders recommend selling one standard deviation below the share price. While it can happen at times, in the majority of cases stock prices are not going to move that much over the lifetime of the options contract.

You can also simply look at probabilities. The closer the strike price is to the share price, the more credit you are going to receive selling the put option. However, the risk that your put option could expire in the money is higher. You can look at delta to get an estimate of the probability that your put option is going to expire in the money, or you can look at the probabilities that your broker has calculated for each option.

It is generally considered safe to sell put options that have a 70% or higher probability of profit.

Keep in mind that if there is a chance that the stock is going to move a lot, you should sit on the sidelines. A good time to sit on the sidelines is immediately after earnings calls, or if there is major event that disrupts the markets.

Otherwise, put options are completely safe to sell.

Brokers will use a formula to determine how much cash that you need to deposit. The amount of cash required is going to be far less than that which would be required to cover buying 100 shares of stock. There are different formulas that are used, and you should check with your broker for the specific formula that they use. This formula is the margin requirement.

In a margin account, margin is the amount of cash that you are required to deposit. A margin account allows you to use leverage. For example, with stock, you can use 2:1 leverage to buy shares of stock. So if you want to buy $20,000 worth of stock, you can put up $10,000 and borrow $10,000 from your broker. In short, when it comes to options trading you have to put up a certain amount of margin – that is deposit a fixed amount of cash, in order to enter into a trade.

Let's say that you were selling a $1225 strike on Google, with shares trading at $1229.50. With an option price of $17 (for a total credit of $1700), you'd have to put up $24,000 in margin.

That is a fraction of the amount you'd need for a protected put on the same trade. For the protected put, you'd have to completely cover the cost of buying 100 shares, and so you'd need to deposit $122,500 into your account.

However, even $24,000 is a lot of money for many people to risk. If that is the case, but you want to get to a point where you are selling naked put options, what you should do is sell put credit spreads in the meantime. The amount of money required to deposit for put credit spreads if much smaller, as we discussed in the previous chapter. So what you can do in that case is trade and buildup your account size until it gets to where it needs to go.

Many people get rich selling naked put options. You can do it too, provided that you are following a careful strategy that involves carefully picking your strike prices, paying attention to the markets throughout the day, and closing your positions when necessary. Avoid picking strike prices that are too near to being in the money.

Selling Naked Calls

Under normal circumstances, traders prefer selling naked put options. However, in a bear market, selling naked call options could be the way to go. You want to be selling call options when you believe that the stock is going to stay at or below the strike price that you select. Obviously you can do this type of trade any time, if there is a share price that you don't believe the stock is going to reach. However, the strategy is best in a bear market of dropping prices.

Selling naked calls is going to require a margin account, just like selling naked puts. There are also going to be specific margin requirements on each option depending on the share price of the underlying stock and the price of the option, as well as the strike price that is used.

When selling naked calls, you are not required to buy the shares of stock ahead of time, in the way that a covered call is setup. So this is a case of having some cash on hand, but not owning the shares. The amount of cash is going to be small in comparison to the amount that would be required in order to buy the shares of stock.

The biggest risk with selling naked options is assignment. To avoid assignment in the case of naked calls, you would use the closing strategy if it becomes necessary. So in this case, what you would be watching out for is the case of rising share prices that could put you in a position of having to sell the shares of stock. If that happens, you can buy your options back to close your position. Once again, this strategy relies on the fact that while an option can be exercised on or before the expiration date, in most cases they are not exercised until expiration.

Conclusion

Thank you for making it through to the end of *Options Trading*, let's hope it was informative and able to provide you with all of the tools you need to achieve your goals whatever they may be.

The next step is to continue your education in options trading and open a brokerage account, and start trading. Start trading in small amounts and work your way up, so that you are not taking reckless risks, but instead building up experience and a sustainable business that can help you reach a zone where you are able to live a life of financial independence. Be sure to read my other books on stock trading, so you can learn about your other possibilities when it comes to trading and investing in the stock market and beyond. Thanks again!

Finally, if you found this book useful in any way, a review on Amazon is always appreciated!

Disclaimer

Please note that *Options Trading,* Jim Livermore, and anyone related to creating this book are not to be held liable for any results that the reader may gain from trading using these strategies. This book is designed for educational purposes only and should be viewed as such by the reader. Any action the reader takes on the information in this book is solely the responsibility and liability of the reader themselves, no one else.

My FREE Gift for You

If you buy my other title, *"Forex Trading Strategy"* I will give you the 2 *"Options Trading + Forex Trading Strategy"* Audiobooks 100% FREE! Forex Trading Strategy is an excellent title that teaches you all about this trading sector. In that fascinating and informative book, we will introduce beginners to the world of Forex trading with step-by-step explanations suitable for beginners. Find out if Forex trading is something suitable for your personality and emotional style, and learn how much money you can make. If you want to get started earning an independent income from trading, don't hesitate to download this book *today.*

What Should I Read Next?

Swing Trading for Beginners: The 2019/20 Valuable Swing Trading Guide for Learning How to Improve Your Trading Results and Your Finances with the Best Low-Risk Approaches

Swing Trading Option: The Ultimate Trading Guide to Discover Safe and Profitable Trading Strategies for Generating Fast and Secure Profits and Rapid Growth for Your Finances

Stocks Option Trading: Learn and Understand How Everything Works and What Pitfalls you MUST Avoid as a Beginner. Learn How Top Investors Lower Their Cost Basis Using Stock Options

Stock Options Trading Strategies: The Best Step-by-Step Guide to Learn How to Trade Stocks and Discover How TOP Traders Invest. The Best Strategies to Help You Create Your Financial Freedom

Forex trading strategy: How to Invest with the Most Profitable and Simple Strategies to Make Money Trading Stocks, Options, Forex, Etfs in 2019 / 2020 Working Just 30 Minutes per Day.

www.ingramcontent.com/pod-product-compliance
Lightning Source LLC
Chambersburg PA
CBHW070338220526
45467CB00001B/169